SHEPHERDING THE SHEEP
Pastoral Care in the Black Tradition

Shepherding the Sheep

Benjamin S. Baker

BROADMAN PRESS
Nashville, Tennessee

© Copyright 1983 • Broadman Press
All rights reserved
4225-43
ISBN: 0-8054-2543-8

Dewey Decimal Classification: 253
Subject Heading: BLACK MINISTERS
Library of Congress Catalog Card Number: 82-73531
Printed in the United States of America

Dedication

To the Saint Stephen Baptist Church, Louisville, Kentucky, and to the Main Street Baptist Church, Lexington, Kentucky—

From the former I was taught Christian ideals as a child, and from the latter I have been challenged to make those ideals real as a man.

Acknowledgments

This writer has borrowed from many sources to make this work what it is.

From my father, the late Percy S. Baker, and mother, Nancy Virenda Baker, I have borrowed their hereditary seed that has been the fertile soil for whatever I have been able to produce.

From my brother, Michael R. Baker, I have borrowed a brother's interest and influence.

From my pastor, the late Dr. B. J. Miller, Sr., I have borrowed the intestinal fortitude to do as he used to say, "Stand on your hind legs and preach the gospel."

From Lincoln Bingham, the superintendent of missions, General Association of Baptists in Kentucky, I have borrowed the enthusiasm and excitement for the ministry of writing.

From Mildred Bailey, I have borrowed her typing skills and analytical reading ability to decipher the secret code of my penmanship.

From my friend, Dr. George C. Wright, assistant professor of history, University of Texas, Austin, Texas, I have borrowed a scholar's search for knowledge and understanding.

From Clarence and Carolyn Day, I borrowed their daughter Carol.

From my wife, Carol, I have borrowed the capacity to give generously and to receive with gratitude.

From my children, Brian Anthony, Beth LaNette, Benne Eunice, and Bennice Carol, I have borrowed the blessings of fatherhood.

BENJAMIN S. BAKER
Lexington, Kentucky

Preface

The intent of this book is to put into the hands of the local pastor or student pastor a resource instrument which will help him in his day-by-day pastoral responsibilities. It has been written, by design and definition, especially for the black pastor, whether or not he has had the opportunity to pursue theological training at an advanced level.

All pastors (ministers) who take seriously the Lord's command, "Feed my sheep," hopefully will be benefited and enlightened by reading this book.

Six basic pastoral models are dealt with in giving the pastor or prospective pastor a clearer perspective of his identity and the role expectations he will need to fulfill as pastor. No pastor should conclude that he has pastoral knowledge because of the longevity of his pastoral ministry. When Jesus invited, "Come unto me" and "Learn of me," he did not mean a season—but a lifetime!

BSB

Contents

SHEPHERDING THE SHEEP
Pastoral Care in the Black Tradition

1
The Pastor as Pastor

I will give you shepherds after my own heart, who will feed you with knowledge and understanding (Jer. 3:15).

The shepherd is the one who provides complete care for all of his sheep. Sheep are helpless (Isa. 53:7), are followers (John 10:3-5), are likely to wander and stray (Isa. 53:6), but under his care they do not lack.[1]

The twenty-third Psalm can be used as a model for how our heavenly Shepherd cares for his flock.

The twenty-third Psalm speaks of:

1. Concern for each individual sheep: "The Lord is my Shepherd" (v. 1). The Good Shepherd calls them by name (John 10:3). He knows them (10:27), and goes out to seek the "one which is lost" (Luke 15:4).
2. Rest: "He makes me lie down" (v. 2). He knows our frame, how much we can handle, what is too much for us and treats us accordingly.
3. Provision for daily sustenance: "green pastures . . . still waters" (food and drink).
4. Refreshment and encouragement when tired, worn or discouraged: "He restores my soul" (v. 2).
5. Guidance and leadership: "He leads [not drives] me" (v. 3). See John 10:3-4: "He calls his own sheep by name and leads them out. . . . He goes before them." See also Revelation 7:17 and Psalm 80:1, "Give ear, O Shepherd of Israel thou who leadest Joseph as a flock!"

6. Instruction, training, and discipline: "He leads me in the paths of righteousness" (v. 3). See 2 Timothy 3:16, "for training in righteousness."
7. Provision for goals and motivation: "for his name's sake" (v. 3).
8. Security and protection: "I fear no evil" (v. 4). His rod and staff protects me. Acts 20:28-30: "Be on guard . . . for all the flock . . . to shepherd the flock of God. . . . After my departure fierce wolves will come in among you, not sparing the flock; and from among your own selves," and John 10:11, when the wolf comes, he "lays down his life for the sheep."
9. Personal fellowship and loving friendship: you are "with me" (v. 4). See John 10:14-15: "I know my own and my own know me, as the Father knows me and I know the Father."

From the wealth of this biblical ore and much more, the Christian minister defines his work as a pastor. It is his task, in following the chief and great Shepherd of the sheep (1 Pet. 5:4; Heb. 13:20), to shepherd God's flock so that they do not lack. That is to say, he must meet their every need.[2]

THE BLACK PASTOR

The black pastor is called upon to be all things to all his people at all times. There are even times when it seems that he is to be more and do more than even the Good Shepherd.

The black pastor's pastoral model is formulated by historical roots, congregational expectations, community expectations, and personal identity.

The black pastor's roots, for the Afro-American pastor, can be traced back to West African rootage. In the West African setting, there was the chief, who was the administrator, organizer, judge, and justice. There was the medicine man who was priest and practitioner. There was the elder who was looked to for wisdom and instruction. There was the witch doctor and conjurers who could remove evil and guilt, and who could get the seeker in touch with the spirits.

The black pastor's formulation on the American soil came as a culmination of these separate and distinct functions into one individual, the pastor. He had to function in a multipurposeful way to meet the needs and expectations of his people.

When Christianity was exposed and taught to the slaves, it had to be acculturated into a form and model that was applicable to their situation. They took their version of Christianity and got what has been called "Blackianity" to suit their unique needs.

The pastor-preacher was called upon not to duplicate the white counterpart, for that role model was too strange and too contradictory for acceptance. What the slave mind needed and requested was a person who could synthesize their West African rootage with the Christian exposure they were receiving. The person who came forth was the black pastor.

The congregational expectation of the black pastor is instrumental in shaping what the black pastor does and does not do.

The congregation looks at their pastor from a patriarchal perspective. He is seen as father or daddy. As such, he is respected and reciprocates that respect by caring for the congregation. There is no area of their lives that is considered off limits to the black pastor.

The black pastor is expected to shepherd the sheep by feeding them, especially with the Word of God. In fact, it has been said that the only thing the black congregation will not forgive the pastor for doing is not preaching. He must preach the Word and do so with vigor and conviction. He has to be diverse enough in his delivery to find both "Aunt Jane" and those in the academic arena.

The community expectations of the black pastor are high because he is seen as the person to lead community causes. In most black communities if the local pastors are not united in dealing with specific issues, usually not much is being done. The depth of how involved the community believes the black pastor ought to be can be seen in the criticism and attacks that are thrown at the black pastor for not addressing himself to particular issues. The frustration comes from the community in that they believe the pastor should be doing something that he is not.

The personal identity of the black pastor is vital in how he does or does not function as a pastor. The first task in this area is for the black pastor to understand who he is. Perhaps the best way to define and declare who the black pastor is would be by attempting to show who he is not. The black pastor is not an incarnated angel who can be everywhere all the time. He is not a superhuman being. He is real flesh and blood, with all of the joy and sadness that comes with being a member of the human drama. The black pastor is not a lord or a ruler, dictating his way and forcing his will upon people. Too many black pastors have an erroneous concept that they are little gods, exerting whatever influence and limited power they have on and over people's lives. The black pastor needs to see himself as an earthen vessel holding a sacred and precious treasure, the Word of God. He needs to see himself as an undershepherd, who by the Good Shepherd, has been given the heavenly charge to care for and feed God's sheep.

The black pastor needs to understand who he is. He is God's child, his servant, his laborer. The black pastor does not belong to the people, though he serves them day and night. He belongs to God who made him, called him, and sent him. He is a man with human limitations but has been given divine authorization to do the Lord's work.

The black pastor should always keep before him *why* he is. He is not for show or style but a servant ready for service. He is not so much to be ministered unto as he is to minister. *He is because God is.* He can do because God is doing.

For the pastor to minister effectively and efficiently he will be called upon to be multifunctional within his position as pastor. Let us consider seven pastoral models from which shepherding the sheep will be a reality.

I feel it necessary to say at the outset that this is not a book about pastoral theology, leadership dynamics, clinical counseling, or the mechanics of organizational structure; but hopefully it is a resource instrument that will help the pastor to pastor.

PASTORAL STYLES

1. *Pastoral Style—Shepherd*
The pastor is the shepherd of the flock. He has been called of God to be the earthly undershepherd, with the responsibility of feeding, leading, and training the sheep in the way the Lord has ordained for his people to follow. The pastor as a shepherd needs to keep in balance that

he is accountable and responsible to Jesus Christ, the Good Shepherd, for the care and handling of his sheep. He is accountable and responsible to the flock for their protection and provisions.

The pastor-shepherd must not forget who he is called to follow, and he must not forget who is to follow him. The picture ought to be one of Jesus Christ, the Good Shepherd, going ahead leading the way, making for both earthly and eternal provisions with the flock of God seeking to follow in his footsteps and the pastor as the undershepherd walking among the sheep, keeping them on course.

For the pastor to shepherd, he must see the sheep. As a pastor you must see your task as serving sheep, God's sheep. The people we serve in pastoral ministry are not pawns to be moved at will or clay to be molded into what we want them to be; neither are they objects to be used for our enjoyment or abuse. They are sheep, God's sheep, and each one is infinitely important in his sight and ought to be in ours.

The psalmist declared, "Know ye that the Lord he is God: it is he that hath made us, and not we ourselves; we are his people, and the sheep of his pasture" (Ps. 100:3, KJV).

The pastor-shepherd must see by keeping in perspective that "the Lord, he is God." Too often pastors feel as though they have been called to do a job that no one else can do or no one else is willing to do. We must remember that the Lord is God. The people we serve, including the good, bad, and indifferent are all the Lord's people. He made them, he knows them, and he cares for them. Our task as pastor-shepherd is not to attempt to figure out God's people or do some miraculous deed in their sight. Our task is to see them as sheep. When we see the flock of God as sheep we will be on our way to having a greater sensitivity (notice I said sensitivity, not understanding) as to why the people we serve as pastors do what they do and think the way they think.

When we see sheep, we ought to be able to see the need and necessity of a shepherd to lead and direct them in the way they should go. Sheep will not go very far without a shepherd. They have not the perspective or analytical ability to discern between green pastures and soggy soil. They are sheep, not soil samplers.

As a pastor-shepherd sees the sheep, he will begin to see his pastoral model of a shepherd in clearer view. There will be several things that he will need to do. He will have to come to them where they are. As has been stated, sheep do not know seek-and-search techniques. Jesus, the Good Shepherd, showed us the necessity of an incarnate ministry. "The Word became flesh and dwelt among us, full of grace and truth; we have beheld his glory, glory as of the only Son from the Father" (John 1:14). As a pastor-shepherd you must go to the sheep where they are, not where you want them to be and not how you want them to be; but where they are is where you must be.

For the pastor to shepherd the sheep, he must be sensitive to the sheep. This is all a part of seeing the sheep. Once you see them and then come to them, you must seek for sensitivity as to where they are, why they are where they are, and what needs to be done to get them where they need to go.

The pastor-shepherd's sensitivity training will come from the Good Shepherd as revealed in God's Holy Word. What the sheep need more than all else is to feed on God's Word. Too often, we as pastors have attempted either to dilute the Word or simply ignore it all together. The tragedy of our actions can apparently be seen in how disobedient, wayward, quarrelsome, and apathetic the sheep become. The basic problem is that they cannot and will not follow if they are hungry. The flock of God does not require tidbits, snacks, and junk food; what the flock needs is a strong, sustaining portion of God's Word.

To be sensitive to the sheep you have to know that they are sheep, see them as such, and then identify with them. As Ezekiel did, you have to sit with them for seven days (Ezek. 3:15). You as pastor may see that they need water, but they will die of thirst unless you calm the waters and still the stream.

You must lead the flock of God into green pastures that are really green, not those that are green because of artificial turf or dye that has been used to cover up the barrenness that is present. We as black people have been both rightly and wrongly accused of getting excited about sensationalism and showmanship. We usually go for the person who talks quick, moves slick, and has a plan for getting rich. The pastor-shepherd must not fall victim to such folly and foolishness.

As the pastor-shepherd sees the sheep, becomes sensitive to the sheep, he then must supply the sheep with grazing pastures.

It is not enough to see the sheep as sheep, be sensitive to what

they need, and then not give them what they need. Your task is to feed
the sheep with the Bread of life and lead them to the stream of
everflowing waters. There can be no substitutions or supplements for
feeding the flock of God. You must not believe that you are the source
or have the resource to supply the needs of the sheep. You do not. Your
shepherd responsibility is to lead and show the way to Jesus Christ, the
Good Shepherd, who can and does supply all of our needs, and who is
sufficient to do more than we could ever ask of him to do.

The pastor-shepherd is the undershepherd, caring for and providing for the flock of God as the Good Shepherd leads his flock to eternal
green pastures.

2. *Pastoral Style—Overseer*

*Take heed therefore unto yourselves, and to all the flock, over the
which the Holy Ghost hath made you overseers, to feed the church of
God, which he hath purchased with his own blood (Acts 20:28, KJV).*

The *episkopos* (an overseer, bishop, pastor) has the responsibility
to *episkopeo* (to oversee).

The pastor-overseer is to oversee the flock of God. The first
responsibility of this pastoral model is for the pastor to take heed unto
himself. He must know *who* he is, *whose* he is, and *why* he is. The
pastor's identity must be God-given and not people-defined. He must
see himself as a pastor with the full meaning of the word. His task is to
feed, care for, lead, and train the flock of God in the life-style the Lord
has ordained for his people to follow.

Take heed to yourself, brother pastor. Make sure you are the
pastor you tell others that you are. There have been too many instances
where a person entered the ministry, especially the pastoral ministry,
before the ministry entered him!

Take heed you are not merely the pastor in name but pastor
because you serve and function as the pastor. You are not the pastor
because you have the title, sit in the pastor's chair, or park in the
pastor's space. You are the pastor only as you pastor. This point is vitally
important for you to understand, as well as for the flock you shepherd.
You owe the congregation responsible leadership because you are the
pastor, called by God, sent and placed by God. The congregation owes
you cooperative fellowship because they are sheep needing a shepherd

to lead them. The highest title any congregation can call the person who serves it is not reverend or doctor—but pastor. The term states that heaven has approved and earth has accepted.

The pastor-overseer has the responsibility of all the ministries of the church. There is no such thing as "this does not concern the pastor," or "he has no business in this matter." If the matter concerns the church, it concerns the pastor. The pastor-overseer must not narrow his perspective down merely to seeing certain areas in the life of the church or dealing with certain departments or auxiliaries. The pastor as overseer has the divinely appointed responsibility of overseeing the whole flock.

The wise pastor will not try to be all things at all times. He will secure a responsible ministerial staff and/or trained persons to serve in specific areas. Even when this is done, it is still the pastor's responsibility to see that all ministries are functioning as they should. Many times it will be heard within the flock by one sheep concerning another, "I do not work in that department," or "It is none of my business or concern what they are doing." The pastor must never think such thoughts or take such an attitude. If he does, he ceases to be the pastor-overseer and becomes the pastor out of touch.

The pastor-overseer will have, for example, a minister of music or designated person(s) to serve with the music ministry of the church. That person will be asked to make musical selections, choir arrangements, help on planning order of services, enlisting new choir members, and so forth; but it is the pastor's responsibility to oversee the music ministry. What is being sung, how it is sung, when and where it is sung is the pastor's responsibility. The pastor cannot take a "cop-out" attitude and say, "I do not handle the music." If he does not do music, he does not do pastoral ministry.

The command in the Scriptures is to take heed to "all the flock." The pastor-overseer must not fragment his pastoral ministry, dealing with certain sheep while ignoring some all together. There will be personality similarities and differences which will make for closeness and distance at the personal level, but the pastor must always strive to relate to his members at the pastor level.

For the pastor-overseer to minister effectively, he needs to pray for godly wisdom and understanding that he may see from the pastoral perspective the flock which he has been called to lead. The pastor-overseer must be "over" his people in the sense that he is aware and knowledgeable of his people. The shepherd must know his sheep and be known by them. He must be aware of both the real needs and the perceived needs of his sheep. The real needs are those things they must have to survive, develop, and grow as sheep of the Good Shepherd's pasture—love, faith, understanding, grace, truth, righteousness, and holiness. The perceived needs are those things the people feel or think they need, that is, padded pews, air-conditioned sanctuaries, choir robes, usher uniforms, and a whole host of niceties which are not essentials. I am not opposed to such things, for I believe the Lord's house ought to be the prettiest house on the block, and his people should present themselves before God fit to come before the King. I simply want to stress the need of a balance in priorities.

The pastor-overseer must feed the flock over which the Holy Ghost has placed him. The pastor's vantage point of overseeing is not to fleece or fault the sheep but to feed them. If one stumbles, he is there; if one or some go astray, he is there; if the entire flock is moving in the wrong direction, he is there with the grace of the Lord to redirect them into their assigned pathway.

The pastor-overseer must see his task as not that of a lord or master but as a servant and colaborer with the people of God. The church belongs to Christ. The people who confess him as Lord and Savior are his. The ministry is his, and the pastor called by him is his.

3. *Pastoral Style—Supervisor*

And when he [Jesus] had called unto him his twelve disciples, he gave them power against unclean spirits, to cast them out, and to heal all manner of sickness and all manner of disease. . . . As ye go, preach, saying, The kingdom of heaven is at hand.
Heal the sick, cleanse the lepers, raise the dead, cast out devils: freely ye have received, freely give (Matt. 10:1,7-8, KJV).

For the pastor-supervisor to minister as he should, he needs to understand the four basic dynamics involved in supervision.

The pastor-supervisor needs to understand the purpose and function of the New Testament church. He will never be able to direct, inspire, inform, and coordinate the multiministries of the church if he does not understand what church is all about.

The purpose and function of the church are evangelism, education, and edification. The evangelistic thrust of the church, plainly stated, is to reach, teach, win, and develop persons for Jesus Christ. This understanding is of the utmost importance as the pastor-supervisor seeks to supervise the flock. He will not know what programs should be allowed and which ones should not. If the program, plan, procedure, or principle cannot fit with the evangelistic mission of the church, it should be seriously considered as to its necessity and whether it is right.

The second function of the church is Christian education. Jesus has commanded us to come unto him and learn of him. The church has the responsibility, in conjunction with the family to teach Christian ideals, practices, and ethics.

The third function is edification. The word *edify* means to build up, to restore, to lift up, and to make stronger. If what is being done or what is being proposed will bring about these desired ends, then they can prayerfully be pursued.

The next dynamic in the supervisor style is the pastor-supervisor. The pastor is the supervisor because he is to have the supervision. He sees beyond what exists now and sees what can and should be.

For the pastor-supervisor to supervise, he must have a healthy self-concept and correct understanding of the purpose and function of the church. If he does not know what the church should be about, he will not know if and when they are about their Father's business.

The self-concept of the pastor-supervisor has to be intact in order for him to minister as a supervisor with pastoral responsibilities. It is the pastor's responsibility to give direction to and leadership for the flock, but he must also be walking and working with the flock. He cannot be in a position of remote control or take a standoff attitude.

The functions of the pastor-supervisor are to enable the workers (sheep) to do their assigned tasks. He does this by helping the member through teaching and training, showing and directing.

The pastor-supervisor's task is to help the member feel the dignity of the task. It is the pastor's responsibility to heighten the worth and usefulness of the member by using them fully to accomplish the ministry of the church. When Jesus called James and John along the

Sea of Galilee they were mending their nets (see Matt. 4:21). This is what the pastor-supervisor must do—mend the nets—not discard them.

The pastor-supervisor's task is to develop personal initiative in the member. Your task as pastor is not to get the person to do the job because it is important to you, but your job, through instruction, is to get the member to see how important and rewarding the job is.

The pastor-supervisor's task is to pledge his encouragement and support. When Jesus called the twelve to be his disciples, he did not tell them what he wanted them to do and then to go and do it by themselves, but he gave them the assurance repeatedly, "I will give you the power, and I will be with you."

The pastor-supervisor will need to provide evaluative techniques for the member who serves in whatever capacity, to see if they are accomplishing the assigned task. He needs to be especially alert in this area, because Christian service cannot be evaluated with the Madison Avenue success scale. Too often good pastors and good people become victims of a worldly standard of success. If we are doing the Lord's work we will have to let him determine by his criteria what kind of job we have done and whether it has been fruitful or not.

The workers, in this case the congregation, will have to be compassionately considered. The pastor-supervisor does not have the right to force or make members of the congregation do the job that needs to be done. For the most part he will be dealing with a volunteer team who will work with him because they love the Lord and are desirous of doing his will and work.

With the congregation (the flock), the pastor-supervisor will have to keep constantly in mind that he is working with sheep, God's sheep, and not a group of little shepherds. Frustration can intensify when the pastor-supervisor sees what needs to be done and then looks to see what appears to be such limited resources to do the job. You must keep in mind, brother pastor, that if the people could do what needs to be done without you, they would not need you as a shepherd.

The tools, the gifts, talents, and skills needed to do the job are always present within the congregation. The Holy Spirit has already equipped the church with the resources and personnel that is necessary to do the job. The pastor-supervisor's task is to pray for the Holy

Spirit to guide and open his eyes that he might truly see. If teaching is to be done, the Holy Spirit has given some the gift of teaching. If mission work, singing, preaching, praying, administrating, healing, discerning, helping, or whatever is needed for the people of God, the church has been so endowed and equipped. The pastor-supervisor will have to tap the fountain and stir those who have the gifts to do the job.

Three Approaches to Supervision: the pastor-supervisor will have to decide which method he will use to accomplish the task.

1. *The Work-Centered Approach:* Authoritarian in nature. The pastor-supervisor enlists or engages persons to do certain jobs, giving them the green light to go ahead and do what needs to be done, based upon the principle that he is the pastor and no further consideration or deliberation needs to be made.

2. *The People-Centered Approach:* democratic in nature. The pastor-supervisor brings the concerns of the congregation before the congregation, gives some direction and offers possibilities and choices for the people to decide which line of action they want to follow. There is usually a vote and what the majority decides becomes the guide for further action.

3. *The Democratic-Authoritarian Approach:* the pastor-supervisor gets the support and approval of the people so that he may go forth and do what needs to be done.

The pastor-supervisor will have to pray for wisdom as to what approach he may use in any given situation. I cannot say any one method is superior to the other, for they all have feasibility in unique situations.

The pastor-supervisor will have to utilize some evaluative instrument to measure the efficient or nonefficient functioning of the assigned task.

There are three areas that the pastor-supervisor will need to evaluate:

Areas to Evaluate

1. *The Structure of the Church Organization:* Is the organizational structure designed to accomplish the desired end? You may have the choir members with beautiful voices, but you will not get a joyful noise unless they are sectionally and vocally

arranged to get the best sound. The pianist, organist, choir director, and all may be doing an excellent job, but the problem may exist in the choir arrangement. This is often for the pastor-supervisor who has the zealous workers and enthusiastic members but may not get the job done because of the church organization. We can be programmed to fail if we are programmed incorrectly.

2. *Process of Action:* How do the leaders and those being led correlate and coordinate their energies to accomplish the assigned task? Many times the pastor-supervisor will have to realistically look to see why a program worked or why it did not work. Personality adjustments have much to do with the progression of an assigned task. Two teachers in the church school may be excellent teachers separately but may not function as team teachers. The pastor-supervisor will have to pray for wisdom in these areas.

3. *The Product or the Fruit of the Labor:* This comes about as a result of the organizational structure functioning correctly and the process of action working as it should. The disciples, when sent out by Jesus, were able to accomplish what he sent them to do when their organizational structure—preaching, teaching, healing—was in line with the process of action, that is, in his name as he had instructed them to do. They brought forth much fruit (the product). Brother pastor, you can still do the same thing if you will supervise.

4. *Pastoral Style—Organizer*

Moses' father-in-law said to him, "What you are doing is not good. You and the people with you will wear yourselves out, for the thing is too heavy for you; you are not able to perform it alone. . . . Moreover choose able men from all the people, such as fear God, men who are trustworthy and who hate a bribe. . . . And let them judge the people at all times; . . . and they will bear the burden with you. If you do this, and God so commands you, then you will be able to endure, and all this people also will go to their place in peace" (Ex. 18:17-23).

These words of Jethro, the father-in-law of Moses, are most

adequate for the pastor-organizer. Too often we have played the role of Moses, sitting from early morning until late at night, listening to the affairs and concerns of our flock and then becoming frustrated because we were not able to do all that needed to be done.

The objective of the pastor-organizer is to organize, arrange, set in order, and fix for action programs for specific purposes and use selected procedures to accomplish the pastoral task.

We as pastors must not think of ourselves or attempt to become one-man bands. We should strive, through God's grace, to be the conductor of the orchestra, getting the best sound for the glory of God.

The pastor-organizer must have the organizational objectives (the church) clarified in his thinking. We do not organize to organize. We organize to function, to bring forth fruit.

All organizational structuring in the church must be biblically based. The church must be seen as the ministering body of Christ. We are many members, yet we are one body. We are one body, yet with many gifts, according as God has given to us (see Rom. 12:3-8; 1 Cor. 12:14; Eph. 4:4-16).

The pastor-organizer will serve most effectively and efficiently when he understands his task, not to do the work of the church but to organize the members of Christ which are the church, to do as Christ has commanded. The organizational philosophy must not be faulty. If we are properly organized, we will then be doing what we should. Too many pastors and churches have overorganized themselves to the extent that the only thing they have is organization—no ministry, no witness, no power, just organization. The organization is a means and not an end.

The pastor-organizer must always check the organizational structure or the proposed organization to see if it is Christ centered. The organization is not there to give someone something to do or to be used as a means of promoting self. The church organization exists as Christ is the center. The picture would be Christocentric and all auxiliaries, departments, committees, programs, and plans evolving out of the expressed command of Christ and revolving around the expressed will of Christ.

A good evaluative instrument which can be used by the pastor-organizer is to ask himself and the church the question, "Is the program or plan being presented in accord with Jesus Christ?"

The pastor-organizer has to structure the organization so it is people centered. There is a genuine danger we can become so programmed and policy and procedure-oriented that we lose sight of why we exist as a church and why we do what we do. Jesus was people-oriented. He opened school on a hill one day to teach people. He made a dining room in Capernaum in the open fields to feed people. He suffered and died on Calvary for people. He took the sting out of death and snatched the victory from the grave—because of people. We, as pastor-organizers, cannot afford to be anything less than people-oriented.

Most of all, the pastor-organizer has to pray and ask the Lord to let both him and the organization be led by the Holy Spirit. We as pastors become aggravated and frustrated many times with the seemingly slow movement and apathetic attitudes of the people of God. We must never forget that they belong to him, and we do too. Thank the Lord for both.

ENLISTING AND INVOLVING SERVANTS FOR THE TASK

Presently we have 20 percent, at best, of our flock doing 80 percent of the church's work. This means overworking some while the great majority of the congregation does nothing. Out of about ten members in any congregation, only about four are involved or engaged in the ministry of the church. We have, either through design or decision, told and taught our people, "Sit down while I stand for you and do the Lord's work for you."

It is a true fact that those who are involved in the church program are for the most part the functional Christians, motivated primarily because of their involvement.

The pastor-organizer will for the most part, especially in the black church setting, have to rely upon volunteer servants to do the job.

I want to share some of the factors as to why some people volunteer when asked, or when there is a need, and some factors which will increase the likelihood of motivation in volunteer servants.

WHY MEMBERS ARE MOTIVATED TO VOLUNTEER

Spiritual Factors. Many members will respond to your appeal to serve in various capacities because they have a sense of divine calling. You as a pastor-organizer need not worry about getting someone to do what needs to be done in the church. Your concern may be discovering or finding that person. The Holy Spirit has already placed the member there.

Leadership Factors. Many members feel capable and adequate to do the job. They will have leadership skills and abilities and will be willing to use these skills in the Lord's service.

Pressure Factors. Many members will respond because the pastor or some other key person asked them to do it. This is OK as long as you honestly give the person asked an opportunity to withdraw respectfully. You do not want a member serving where he or she does not really want to be.

Personal Factors. The member will usually serve if a personalized approach is made. Mass appeals usually do not work over a long period of time. Asking everybody is almost like asking nobody.

Educational Factors. The member may have or think they have expertise or competence in a certain area. You should not think that just because a person has advanced secular training or education he or she will be ideal. Oftentimes just the reverse is true.

Promise Factors. Members serve often in hopes or promise of receiving reward or recognition. We all should serve to hear the Master say, "Well done."

FACTORS WHICH INCREASE THE LIKELIHOOD OF MOTIVATION AND PARTICIPATION OF VOLUNTEERS

1. There has to be confidence in the skills and motives of the leader. If you present yourself as a competent pastor-organizer with definite plans and directives, people will usually follow. There is nothing worse than a wandering sheep following a wandering shepherd.

2. The program goals must be those with which the people can identify. As a pastor-organizer you have to do more than just believe the idea will work. You have to convince others that it will work.

3. You should be seen as a colaborer. Very few people are going to do volunteer work while you sit and watch them. Jesus did not have the disciples doing something he was not doing.

4. Encourage enthusiasm and excitement. Enthusiasm is contagious. Get it and spread it.

5. Furnish proper reinforcement and praise. A person who is praised and shown the consequences of a job well-done will be more likely to become involved than someone who is asked to do something without any consideration or reward for their efforts.

6. Explain all these: effective communication between what is being asked, how it is to be done, why it is being done, who will help, and the time and effort involved to complete the task. Nothing will turn a person off quicker than asking them to do something that you are not too sure about. Anticipate the questions before they are asked, and give solutions and directions before the problem presents itself.

7. Use inclusive and plural language. Learn to say, "We are going to do" rather than "I want you to do." Let the potential volunteer know that others will help, and they are not being asked to do something no one else will do.

5. Pastoral Style—Enabler

And he gave some, apostles; and some, prophets; and some, evangelists; and some, pastors and teachers; For the perfecting of the saints, for the work of the ministry, for the edifying of the body of Christ (Eph. 4:11-12, KJV).

When Christ ascended to the Father, "he led a host of captives, and he gave gifts to men" (Eph. 4:8). These "gifts" of the Spirit are to enable the church to become a ministering body of Christ.

For too long and too often in the black church, the pastor has been called upon to do the work, ministry, mission, and maintenance of the church. There were, and still are, a few pastors around who believe it is their task to do everything. Let us look at the biblical bases for the pastor-enabler to be utilized in pastoral ministry.

We first need to define gifts and the fruit that comes from the application of the gifts.

Gifts are the consequence of the presence of the Holy Spirit given to equip the children of God. The church, as the body of Christ, is not powerless, nor does it have a shortage of members to do the task that it has been assigned. The Holy Spirit has already given gifts to the body of Christ to carry out its mission efficiently and effectively.

The gifts are the manifestation of the Holy Spirit through the believer to make Christian service effectual. Without the Holy Spirit so equipping and empowering, the Christian would be ineffective. The key understanding here for the pastor-enabler is to know that the Holy Spirit has equipped and is working through the believer to do the job. What is the scope of these gifts?

There is a variety of gifts.

In Romans 12:3-8, these gifts are:

1. Prophecy
2. Ministrations
3. Teacher
4. Exhortation
5. Giver
6. Ruler
7. He who shows mercy

In 1 Corinthians 12:8-10, these gifts are:

1. Utterance of wisdom
2. Utterance of knowledge
3. Faith
4. Healing
5. Miracles
6. Prophecy
7. Discernment of spirits
8. Interpretation of tongues

In 1 Corinthians 12:28, these gifts are:

1. Apostles
2. Prophets
3. Teachers
4. Workers of miracles
5. Healers
6. Helpers (serviceable ministries)
7. Government (administrators)
8. Varieties of tongues

In Ephesians 4:11, these gifts are:

1. Apostles
2. Prophets
3. Evangelists
4. Pastors and teachers

Spiritual gifts have a twofold purpose: to strengthen the church's fellowship and extend the church's witness and ministry.[3]

Certainly Paul's words in 1 Corinthians 12:1 should be brought to the prayerful attention of every pastor-enabler, "It is important, brethren, that you should have clear knowledge on the subject of spiritual gifts."

The pastor-enabler's task is to equip, enable, give training and leadership to the members of the congregation to carry out the mission of the church.

To do this, the pastor-enabler needs to be aware of the sources of potential leadership. We have stated that what is needed to do the job is already present. It is a matter of discovering and enlisting them into active service.

SOURCES OF LEADERSHIP

The pastor-enabler must analyze and determine the church's needs for leadership. The needs of the church will tell us much about how many leaders are needed.

This would include an analysis of existing leadership vacancies, as well as a study of anticipated turnover of leadership within the next year or so. Once the needs and vacancies are thoroughly identified, Crossland suggests the church do a "job analysis" on each of the vacancies and anticipated vacancies. In developing a job analysis, such questions ought to be asked concerning a particular job: What is the purpose of this job? How does it fit into the total program of the church? What other tasks are related to it? What are the chief duties? How much time is involved?[4] When these and similar questions are answered, the church "will have a reasonably accurate idea of the kind of person" they are seeking, as well as discovering how many leaders they need or soon will need.

This leads us to the next step, the matching of talents to church positions. But where do we find the people? What are the sources of leadership? Crossland believes the *entire membership* of the church should be studied in a member-by-member search for leaders.[5] Philip Harris also suggests scanning the names in a church directory as a valuable tool for discovering potential leaders.[6] Another source of leadership is the new member orientation class and new members in general. The director may be able to recommend qualified people who have recently transferred their membership into the church.[7] Still another source can be church members holding positions of leadership in professional, civic, or social organizations within the community, who do not hold positions of leadership in the life of the church. Philip

Harris states that many churches appoint scouts who search for such leaders.[8] Many times such community leaders have never become involved in church work because they have never been asked.

Another area of leadership potential is with the youth. Youth projects can be a tremendous means by which a church can become aware of youth leadership ability.

Parents are often a rich source of children's leadership. When a church is actively seeking to minister to the needs of its children, no apology should be made for asking the help of parents.[9]

Another place to find potential leaders is in the regular attenders. Jimmy Crowe suggests that discovery groups be formed to challenge those who have fallen off on attendance to become part of a special study group that might meet during Sunday School.[10] This course would be led by a capable teacher with sensitivity to spotting future leaders.

Crossland suggests four more sources.[11] First, the pastor and staff calling on members and prospects for membership will often offer good leads. Then, the choir and other musical groups in the church can be drawn upon for directors or music leaders for the total musical program of the church. Still another source offered by Crossland is former church leaders, not presently holding office. Careful consideration should be given to this group of individuals. Some may have quit because they were placed with the wrong age group or because they received little or no support in a role new to them. Perhaps a temporary health, job, or family problem long since resolved may have hindered success. Obviously, many of these former leaders may be ready to serve again in a most capable manner. Good record keeping, it should be noted, is a prerequisite to a successful search for former leaders.

Finally, retired persons provide a great reservoir of untapped skill and experience. Many retirees possess the time, abilities, and willingness to undertake church leadership positions. Former teachers, secretaries, and business persons are just a few of the talent areas that can be utilized.

Whatever methods are used, whatever sources are tapped for securing leaders to fill present and anticipated vacancies, "an adequate filing system for recording and retaining information on prospective leaders is essential."[12]

Let us now turn to the actual searching for person power.

SEARCHING FOR PERSON-POWER

Jimmy Crowe, the late Gaines S. Dobbins, and others proposed the all-important concept of the priesthood and servanthood of every believer. Dobbins pointed out that Christ made spiritual leaders out of men who were not leaders in the eyes of the world, men who accepted Christ's concept of leadership as servanthood. Crowe elaborates on this concept by pointing out that every Christian is meant to be this sort of leader:

> In the New Testament all believers are called the priests of God. Priesthood by its very nature involves leadership. Therefore, all of God's people should be looked upon as potential leaders. The New Testament concept of the priesthood is one of leadership, and leadership is that of servanthood, ministry, humility, and example. Leadership, as seen in the New Testament is "loving service." It opens wide the gates of fulfillment, influence, and leadership to every Christian.[13]

Thus, the search for Christian leadership should extend to every believer and should include their development as servants of Christ.

Even as every believer should be seen as a potential leader, some criteria for selection of organizational leaders should be formulated so as to search wisely.

Dobbins gives a helpful list of essential qualifications:

> Lists of leadership qualifications usually include physical and mental health; . . . above-average intelligence; . . . clearly defined aims; contagious enthusiasm; perseverance in the face of discouragement; ability to learn and willingness to share; good reputation and integrity of character; devotion to the task and loyalty to the cause.[14]

> Worthy qualities which a Christian leader should possess are as follows: loyalty to Christ, love for the church, devotion to the work of the church, regular attendance, personality, ability to work with others, integrity, leadership ability, willingness to handle responsibility, good judgment, good reputation, and

talent appropriate to the task.[15]

Having looked at the qualities to be considered in potential leaders, let us now look at some of the ways we might search for leaders with the development of leaders. Every effort must be made to encourage organizational heads and committee chairpersons to share their leadership responsibilities with those whom they supervise. "In doing so [the leader] acquaints these people with the leadership roles in organization, has an opportunity to give some personal training and creates situations in which he can observe them."[16]

Margaret Sharp suggests that in every search for leaders, a very important ingredient is prayer for the guidance of the Holy Spirit. As she so aptly states: "The Holy Spirit will do more than match names to jobs. He will work in the hearts of those who should accept leadership positions."[17]

Finally, consider the talent survey. A survey can be conducted through the Sunday School to secure such information as experience, interests, and willingness to train. With new members, a talent survey can be taken whenever they join the church. A general survey can be given to the entire congregation to secure potential leaders.

ENLISTMENT

The pastor-enabler, if he is effective, will have to discover and then enlist members to do the necessary work.

The basic plan recommended to help the pastor-enabler in his task, for the cultivation and enlistment of volunteer church leaders, was presented by Jimmy Crowe. The plan is simple, fundamental, and practical. It can be administered by a volunteer lay leader or by a professionally trained church staff member.

Eight Steps in Church Leader Enlistment

Step 1: *Begin with Prayer.* This plan of enlistment depends upon the Lord's help and leadership. Without the guidance of the Holy Spirit, there is no guarantee of success. Throughout the endeavor of enlisting adults for service, "Pray without ceasing" (1 Thess. 5:17, KJV).

Step 2: *Make a List.* Before you can successfully enlist adults for service, you need a list of people with which to work. "Ask, and it shall be given you; seek, and ye shall find; knock, and it shall be opened unto you" (Matt. 7:7, KJV).

Step 3: *Build the Prospective Leader's Self-Confidence.* Most prospective workers need to develop a greater degree of self-confidence before they will even give a second thought to becoming a worker. Some people have a genuine fear of the leadership role. It is therefore necessary for the person using this plan to build the self-confidence of those persons he has enlisted as potential workers. Your personal guiding principle should be, "For God hath not given us the spirit of fear; but of power, and of love, and of a sound mind" (2 Tim. 1:7, KJV).

Step 4: *Mention the Possibility of Working with the Age Group.* Remember, this is not the time to ask for a definite commitment to service. It is simply the planting of a thought. Commitment comes later. When ready, tell the prospective worker that you believe he or she can become an excellent leader with the chosen age group. Paul reminded us that although we may till the soil and plant the seed, still it is "God that giveth the increase" (1 Cor. 3:7, KJV).

Step 5: *Lead the Prospect to Observe in Structured Situation.* Observers should have no responsibilities whatsoever during these sessions. They are there to get a feel of what is going on in a particular situation, seeing how it is being done and what can be done to improve it. They are there to look, listen, and learn.

Step 6: *Enlist the Potential Worker in Your Leader Training Program.* All of the previous preparation and work come to focus in this final step. Enlist the individual in the leader training program. It will be easier to enlist the prospective workers to begin training than to enlist them to begin working. Make it clear that at this time you are not asking him to take a job. You are asking him to prepare for service. There are no strings attached. There is no obligation when the training program is completed.

Step 7: *Commit to Service.* When the trainee has completed her training, you should be prepared to discuss a specific place of service.

Step 8: *Continue Training and Follow-Up.* During the first six to eight weeks, a worker sometimes becomes disillusioned and discouraged. Prevent this by maintaining close contact during this period. Check frequently on his progress. Offer suggestions.

GETTING THE SERVANT COMMITTED TO THE TASK

The pastor-enabler will have the entire congregation to choose from as potential servants to do the job of ministering. He will need to be aware of the four levels of action.

4	**CONSENT**
3	**COMPROMISE**
2	**ASSENT**
1	**ACQUIESCENCE**

The first level is acquiescence. This is when the pastor-enabler gets the potential worker's attention about the situation. That is what God had to do with Moses. The Lord got Moses' attention by manifesting himself in a burning bush (Ex. 3:2).

The second step is assent. Begin to move the potential worker toward positive action. The Lord told Moses that he would send him forth, and he would be with him.

The third step is compromise. This is the area that differences are worked out. When the Lord told Moses that he was going to send him to lead the deliverance of the children of Israel, Moses stated he was not adequate for the job. The Lord assured him that he would be with him, and he would have Aaron to help him speak.

The fourth step is consent. This is the point where you get the worker to agree to do the job that is asked of him or her. After the rough spots have been worked out, you are then in a position to move forward positively.

In conclusion, the pastor-enabler, to be successful, must discover and enlist lay leaders in the church. To do this effectively, it is necessary to keep certain factors in mind. The pastor-enabler, along with the church, must determine whether or not it needs more leaders and what kind of leaders it wants. This necessitates a careful analysis of its leadership needs. Then the pastor-enabler must get in touch with all of the sources he has at his fingertips. Next, the pastor-enabler and the church must consider some basic qualities that are desired in its leaders and conduct the leadership search. Once prospects have been identified, the actual enlistment begins. Enlistment is always tailored to the individual prospect for a specific church position.

Above all, good records should be kept throughout the whole enlistment process and Christ's leadership should be sought.

6. Pastoral Style—Administrator

For though I be free from all men, yet have I made myself servant unto all, that I might gain the more. To the weak became I as weak, that I might gain the weak: I am made all things to all men, that I might by all means save more (1 Cor. 9:19,22, KJV).

Certainly these words of Paul express the diverse and multifunctional role that the black pastor-administrator has had to perform. It can be said that the black pastor is *the* administrator for the black church. As he goes, so goes the church, and as he does, so things happen.

Most administration in black churches seems to be run by the grace of God and the mercy of the people, without adequate records, permanent paid employees . . . We have lost many members on the basis that we never use them in the church structure unless they can be used for the personal benefit of the minister and of his administration.[18]

In spite of many recent economic gains experienced in the black community, the black church constituency is comprised of the "organized poor," who lack financial resources and the power to change their condition. Nonetheless, community expectations require the church to meet the needs presented to them. The situation of the black church is similar to that of Jesus of Nazareth when confronted by five-thousand hungry men with only five barley loaves and two small fish supplied by a little lad (John 6:9).[19]

If the black pastor-administrator is to serve in this capacity, he needs to understand for what purposes one attempts to administer the operation of the church. The mechanics of church administration are mastered in vain unless they are exercised in a spirit of love and togetherness.[20]

The Pastor-Administrator: a Definition

Administration is the task of discovering and clarifying the goals and purpose of the field it serves and of moving in a coherent, comprehensive manner toward their realization. Such a definition suggests certain questions that any administrator must frequently ask: What end or goal is to be served? What means will help reach the goal? How can all available resources and leadership be utilized in a coordinated and comprehensive movement toward the goal?[21]

The pastor-administrator must have a biblical-based understanding of the purpose and mission of the New Testament church. He will not function correctly as an administrator unless he realizes his task and has some understanding of how to go about fulfilling his administrative responsibilities.

The means must be kept in perspective as to the goal that has to be reached. The pastor-administrator must not become victimized by having an "active program" in the church and, in reality, be far from the purpose of what the church is to be about. There are too many pastors and too many churches that are simply busy doing and accomplishing nothing. Jesus was busy, but he was about his Father's business.

The programs, plans, and procedures that are used must be in keeping with the mission and purpose of the church. That mission and purpose is to evangelize, educate, and edify. If the pastor-administrator seeks or strives to propose anything that is not in keeping with the New Testament church's objective, it should be seriously questioned.

Once the pastor-administrator has clarified his goals and objectives, he moves to the second step of defining what means will help in reaching the desired goal. The pastor-administrator clarifies and defines where it is he is trying to go. He then has to define and clarify the possible means or ways of getting to where he wants to go. The means must never become ends in themselves but simply means to obtain the desired goals. If, for example, the pastor-administrator is striving to develop the church with an evangelistic thrust, he first must understand the purpose and objectives of evangelism. Secondly, he must define the means that are at his disposal that can be used to bring about the end result.

The third area of vital concentration for the pastor-administrator is coordinating all of the available resources and leadership possibilities toward the desired goal. The Holy Spirit has equipped the church with the actual and potential persons to do the ministry of the church. The pastor-administrator's challenge is to discover, enlist, and utilize the resources that are available. There are too many situations where the pastor and the congregation have erroneously concluded that what and who is needed to do the job is not present or available. Be assured, brother pastor, the person(s) is there. You will have to pray for guidance and sensitivity to discover the resources and the resource person(s).

The pastor-administrator may have all of the resources and all of the necessary persons to do the job, but the test of his administrative skills will come in coordinating, correlating, and communicating all of the components into a harmonious composite to get the job done.

The Qualifications of the Pastor-Administrator

The pastor is not the pastor just because he is called the pastor. He is the pastor when and as he pastors. The pastor-administrator is such when he administers the affairs of the church.

For the pastor-administrator to be efficient and effective, he must be able to share his views and beliefs with the church that he serves. It is not sufficient for the pastor-administrator to know what the goals and objectives are if no one else does. When he administers without the group or the church's understanding of what is being done and why it is being done, he functions alone. If the pastor-administrator wants to be a one-man band, then he can do it this way; but he will not last very long, and his work will be only marginal at best.

The pastor-administrator has to share through teaching, training, and telling the flock what it is the church ought to be about and how we should be about it. The pastor-administrator should think of himself as a conductor of the orchestra, assuring that the best possible sound will be heard.

Too often the pastor-administrator has assumed all of the responsibility, and when the attempted assignments are not successful no one is discouraged or disappointed but him. Learn to share your pastor-administrative work. You are not a specialist in everything. You are a shepherd with the responsibility of feeding the sheep.

The pastor-administrator should have a genuine love for people. Pastors are in a people business. People are our premium, people are our priority, people are our purpose. You will not be a pastor-administrator if you do not have compassion and concern for people. In fact, you will not be much of a pastor if you do not have a genuine love for people.

The pastor-administrator must be biblically based and Christ centered in his administrative approach. We too often get sidetracked according to the world's standards of success (large offering + large attendance = success). For the pastor-administrator to serve well, he must do it the biblical way. There are thousands of books, pamphlets, and articles written each year on methodologies, approaches, techniques, and procedures; but there still is no source book that comes close to giving instructions as to how the church is to be administered other than the Bible. The pastor-administrator's technique and how-to skills must come from the Bible. That is the only way that he knows that what he is doing is God approved and thus right.[22]

The Procedures in Pastoral Administration

There are about eight basic process steps that are important in effective church administration. The pastor-administrator needs to be at least aware of these and move toward implementing them in his particular situation. I feel I should say again that the attempt of this work is not to write extensively about church administration but to put a resource instrument into the hands of the pastor to help him shepherd the sheep.

The administrative process would include:

Process One: Recognition of Need

Before any pastoral administrative work can begin, the pastor needs to recognize and specifically state what the need is. If the need is motivation of the group or the entire church, then he has to start there. If the need is cooperation or organizing or simply coming to a joint understanding, then that has to be the starting point.

Process Two: Planning

Once the need has been defined and localized, determine what persons or resources will be necessary to meet the need or see that it is eliminated. Planning is quite essential to the pastor-administrator because without a plan, you may have all of the right ingredients and all of the right materials but no guide to follow.

Process Three: Organizing

Organizing involves getting the persons and the materials together to work toward the defined objective. You may have members with beautiful voices, and your church may have beautiful musical instruments, but you will have only at best a joyful noise unless they are organized and harmonious.

Process Four: Staffing

After the need has been discovered and defined, plans are put into operation and an organizational structure is developed. The staffing consists of who will be needed to accomplish the task. Do we have such a member presently in our congregation who can do the job? Will we have to train and develop members for the task? Is this for short duration or for long-range and permanent purposes? These questions and many more will have to be seriously asked and answered.

Process Five: Directing

Usually the pastor-administrator will give the major direction to the administrative task. He must not, however, attempt to lead alone. He needs the leadership, input, and support of others, for one can only lead as he can get others to follow. The pastor-administrator's directing will come at many points. Sometimes the situation will call for him to be out front, sometimes in the middle and sometimes behind. When he has done his job well, he will be able to turn over many of the administrative chores to others to carry out.

Process Six: Coordinating

In this process, the pastor-administrator will have to pull together all of his available resources and persons and blend them together in such a way that each person can make a contribution to accomplish the task. The pastor-administrator should keep in his mind that each member of the congregation has something to offer, no matter how small or insignificant it might seem.

Coordinating takes place when the goals and objectives of the pastor-administrator become socialized and internalized into being the goals and aspirations of the group.

Your task as pastor-administrator is not to get other persons to work on your programs, but to get the people of God to work for his glory and honor.

Process Seven: Communicating

It is not enough for you to understand the nature and mission of the church. You have to communicate through teaching and showing what that nature and mission is.

To communicate, you have to send a clear and understandable message. The receivers, in this case the congregation in general or a group in particular, have to interpret and apply the message as it has been received.

There is no way that you can conclude that you have communicated once and for all. You will have to constantly check to make sure that what you are trying to get across is what the group or member is receiving.

The pastor-administrator must never assume that everyone knows what he is talking about or what his plans are no matter how plain or simple they may seem to him.

Process Eight: Budgeting

There is a cost factor involved in pastoral administration. The cost factor may be expressed through time, talent, or tithe. It may take the form of money, means, or materials. The pastor-administrator must watch and pray that he does not turn from doing a biblically-based program or a Christ-centered command simply because he or others lead him to believe that the cost is too great. The Lord does not command us to do things and lead us by his spirit and then tell us, "If you do not have the money or the materials, just forget it." With every God-centered program he provides the means, materials, and money.

Budgeting should also take into consideration the time factor. Our God is a timely God, and we are timely creatures. We have to develop the discipline of proper time usage. The Lord has already given the time for us to do what he wants us to do. We must set goals, have clear perspectives, and work within a time frame to accomplish the task.

Nothing will discourage members any quicker than to have a plan or a program that has no sense of time or direction. We realize that we are going to study the Bible the rest of our lives, but we cannot start a Bible study with a book of the Bible, a theme, or a doctrine and say, "We'll study this from now on."

THE EVALUATION OF PASTORAL ADMINISTRATION

These eight evaluative questions are given by Alvin J. Lindgren in *Foundations for Purposeful Church Administration*:

1. What are the goals toward which the activity is supposedly moving?
2. Are these goals in harmony with the nature and mission of the church?
3. Will the activity contribute to achieving the goals?
4. Is the activity in conflict with any other equally valid project of the congregation?
5. Are sufficient personnel and resources available to carry out the activity? Or will the congregation be overburdened by it?

6. Will all the techniques employed bear examination in the light of the gospel?

7. Is there a danger that this activity, as a means to an end, will become an end in itself, thus obscuring the real goal by its very "success"?

8. Are there other more basic goals that require prior attention?[23]

The pastor-administrator will have to evaluate what he is doing in the here and now with the church over which the Holy Spirit has made him overseer. One day he will have to stand before the judgment seat of Christ and give an account for every deed that he has done.

7. Pastoral Style—Counselor

Come now, and let us reason together, saith the Lord: though your sins be as scarlet, they shall be as white as snow; though they be red like crimson, they shall be as wool (Isa. 1:18, KJV).

WHAT PASTORAL COUNSELING IS

Pastoral counseling differs from other counseling in one major respect, namely, the inclusion of the religious dimension. "The goal of spiritual counseling is to bring men and women into right relationship with God and to lead them into the abundant life."[24] To save in the Greek means to heal or make whole; therefore, salvation is wholeness, soundness, deliverance from everything that blights and warps human personality and prevents fellowship with God.

The task of the pastor in pastoral counseling is to bring help to the tempted and spiritual renewal to the defeated. The pastor-counselor must always have his identity in perspective. He is the pastor, not the psychologist or personality analyst. He will have to bring in many of the skills and techniques used by professional counselors, but he must not, however, assume the role of being what he is not. All pastoral counseling should be done within the pastoral context. The pastor is concerned in his counseling with a member of the flock. He must continuously hear Jesus' words to Peter, "Do you love me? Feed my sheep" (John 21:15-17). The pastor-counselor is called upon to do just that, feed the sheep. The pastor-counselor will be tempted to fault the sheep, fleece the sheep, and even forfeit the sheep. He must understand his responsibility is to compassionately care for the sheep as Jesus Christ, the Good Shepherd, guides and gives him grace to do the task.

The task of the pastor-counselor is to: comfort those who are troubled; give guidance to the perplexed; bring "deliverance to the captives"; give assurance of forgiveness to the penitent; give courage to the sick and bereaved; recovery of sight to the blind; and to meet the personal needs of the members who comprise the congregation.

The function of the counseling relationship will be twofold: 1. To strengthen the ego, or the self, or the conscious functions of a person through which the integrative, maturing processes are achieved (the human dimension), and 2. To appropriate the spiritual resources that God offers (the divine dimension).

The first function of the pastor-counselor is to get the members in touch with themselves and come to a clear perspective of their identity. This is vitally important, especially so in the black context.

Certainly one of the sources of black people's dilemma rest in their unhealthy and distorted personal identities. They have been programmed and "procedurized" so long that they have lost touch with who they are. Their identities have been shaped for them and to a great extent, they simply function out of those false and imaginary identities.

The second task of the pastor-counselor is to utilize the spiritual resources that God offers. For black people, the point of concern is for them to realize whose they are. The black pastor-counselor must be sensitive and aware that his parishioners will, for the most part, not know or remember this crucial identity situation. It matters not what others say, do, or think as long as I know I am a child of the King. The King's children just behave in a different way, and they have some peculiar resources at their disposal.

The pastor-counselor must be aware that a true counseling situation does not necessarily exist when a pastor and a parishioner are engaged in conversation together. Counseling is not the mere exchange of words. A need must be known by the counselee, and he must see the need of receiving assistance in solving the problem that is troubling him.

Seward Hiltner wrote that a true counseling situation exists when a parishioner recognizes that something is wrong, senses that this is in some measure within him, and is convinced that a professional person may be able to help him with it, not by giving him the answer but by helping him to clarify it for himself.[25]

THE PROCESS OF PASTORAL COUNSELING

There are three factors which affect the approach of the minister toward counseling: (1) his attitudes toward persons and their problems, (2) his religious interpretations of man, and (3) his conception of himself and of his role as a minister. These factors determine the course and quality of the counseling process.[26]

The pastor-counselor's attitudes toward members of the flock will affect how he relates to them as pastor and how they will relate to him. If the pastor-counselor's attitude is one of authoritarian paternalism where he has to be looked upon as the father with all of the correct answers, many members will feel threatened to even share their problems and burdens. The pastor-counselor should always strive to maintain the level of human touch where the members' hurt can be identifiable with the pastor, and the pastor can identify with the members. God, through Christ, showed us the significance of this in that he became like us, yet without sin.

The pastor-counselor's understanding of man will greatly influence his approach and his attitude during the counseling situation. If his interpretation of man is one of contempt and disgust, he will view every counseling situation as just a part of the human drama that surely will happen to mortal creatures.

If on the other hand his interpretation of man is viewed as understanding man made in the image of God with moral responsibility and personal accountability, he will confront the counseling situation as a challenge to bring out the best in man through the grace of God.

The pastor-counselor's self-concept has to be healthy in that he understands himself and is in touch with his own emotions and feelings.

If the pastor-counselor conceives of himself as having or supposedly having all of the answers to life's questions, he will do a drastic disservice in his counseling situations.

If he conceives of himself as a real person with real strengths and weaknesses, with some answers and many questions, he will be at the point of human contact that is needed to assist the counselee in search for understanding.

James D. Hamilton, in *The Ministry of Pastoral Counseling*, lists seven functions of counseling. I want to share them at this point, for I believe them to be most helpful in assisting the pastor-counselor to shepherd the sheep.[27]

1. *Listening.* One of the greatest assets the pastor-counselor can utilize is his ability to listen. You will not be in a position to give assistance to the counselee until you have first heard what they are saying. So many people just need someone to hear them out, to compassionately consider what is happening in their lives, and to respond in a loving, caring way.

2. *Responding.* The pastor-counselor should be aware that he does not respond prematurely, answering the question without fully understanding. The response should be in the affirmative, giving definite responses, and yet it should leave room for questions and clarity.

3. *Supporting.* In the supporting task, the pastor-counselor is to uplift and sustain the member. This does not mean to agree with the counselee in an area where there is disagreement, or to tell them they are right when they are wrong. It does mean to bear with the counselee, supporting them even though the issue or the behavior may be indifferent.

4. *Clarifying.* This is crucial. One of the dangers of the counseling situation is for the counselor and the counselee to erroneously conclude that they have heard one another and understood one another, when in reality they have not. To clarify, the pastor-counselor will have to restate what is being said to make sure correct communication is taking place.

5. *Interpreting.* Here is where the situation can be clarified and then investigated to see how and what can be done to rectify it. For the pastor-counselor, this is the point of presenting choices and options and

for the counselee, this is the point of decision. The pastor-counselor should be especially sensitive that he does not answer or make the choice for the counselee.

6. *Formulating.* Once a decision has been made on the best course of action, the pastor-counselor will need to help the counselee formulate or arrange the necessary attitude and action that will be needed to carry out the decision.

7. *Guiding.* This is the point of walking with the counselee through the new pastures. Sensitivity and sense, with the Holy Spirit's guidance, will have to be used as to how much and how long this walk should last.

Do's and Don'ts for the Pastor-Counselor

DO'S

1. Be a pastor-counselor. You are a pastor with counseling responsibilities, not vice versa.
2. Be a good listener. Many answers are in the question. Listen for it.
3. Be sensitive to nonverbal language. Facial expressions, body language, eye contact, the counselee's emotions.
4. Be confidential. The counselee is inviting you into an intimate part of life. Respect it as such.
5. Set a time limit for the counseling situation. Usually this is about an hour maximum.
6. Keep a record of the counseling situation and progression file. Previous information can help you in the present and future.
7. Do rely upon the guidance of the Holy Spirit to lead you that you may lead members of the flock.

DON'TS

1. Don't attempt to be a professional counselor unless you have specialized training.
2. Don't evaluate the situation without knowing the facts.
3. Don't inject your problem(s) with that of the counselee.
4. Don't condemn the counselee, even though he may be

wrong. Your task is to compassionately correct and pastorally direct the counselee in the right direction.

5. Don't be aggressive toward the counselee. Let her talk. You listen.

6. Don't treat the counseling situation as unimportant. No matter how small or insignificant the situation may seem to you, to the counselee it is major.

7. Don't give false hope. If you cannot help the counselees yourself, you can help by referring them to someone who can.

The pastor is called upon to counsel. He is not a psychologist, psychiatrist, or a clinical counselor. He is a pastor and that is enough. He must see himself as a pastor with counseling responsibilities. His personal identity, religious interpretation of man, and his attitude toward people will greatly enhance or hinder his pastoral-counseling ministry.

The skills that are needed to be an effective pastor-counselor are really quite simple: the Holy Spirit's guidance, sense, and sensitivity.

2

The Pastor as Preacher

There was a man sent from God, whose name was John. The same came for a witness, to bear witness of the Light, that all men through him might believe (John 1:6-7, KJV).

How then shall they call on him in whom they have not believed? And how shall they believe in him of whom they have not heard? and how shall they hear without a preacher? And how shall they preach, except they be sent? as it is written, How beautiful are the feet of them that preach the gospel of peace, and bring glad tidings of good things! (Rom. 10:14-15, KJV).

BRIEF HISTORY OF BLACK PREACHING

Historical Records

The first historical record of black preachers reflected the belief that they were either Baptists, Methodists, or Congregationalists. This can be attributed to the fact of their association and assimilation with their white counterparts. The slave preacher was a unique combination of West African origin and white American church structure. You cannot begin to understand the black preaching development or the black religious experience without being acutely aware of West African religion on the one side and the white American church on the other. The black church, the black worship experience, and black preachers are all a composite of both. For the slave preacher to be effective, he had to meet certain basic qualifications. They were, namely:

1. *His ability to demonstrate and declare that he had been "called" of God to do that which he was doing.* It was the "calling"

55

which set the preacher miles apart from his peers and the "calling" authorized him to speak on God's behalf. No serious person, be they religious or not, would question the authenticity of the slave preacher if he testified the Lord had "called" him to preach. The ultimate test, however, as to whether he was genuine came out in his ability or his inability to preach. I can recall even my pastor, the late Dr. B. J. Miller, Sr., saying, "The worst thing a man can do is say the Lord has called him to preach, and then not be able to preach." As the years pass on I agree more readily than ever before.

2. *His possession of some biblical knowledge.* He did not have to be a theological giant or a scholarly, biblical exegete, but he did have to demonstrate at least his exposure to the biblical text. Oftentimes he quoted what he heard or made a certain text say what he wanted it to say. Very seldom was his word questioned as to the meaning or usage of a particular passage of Scripture. The slave preacher was a master in the art of diversification. He could use one passage of Scripture one way in a certain situation and then turn it completely around to be used in another.

3. *His ability to "tell the story."* He had to have something to say, and he had to have the ability to say it. The only thing the slave preacher, and even the black preacher today, was not and will not be forgiven for is not preaching. He had to "tell the story" so the biblical Word became incarnated in him, living with new and vivid meaning.

4. *His ability to sing.* Often, when he could not speak, he had to sing it out. This kind of preaching was characterized by "short songs." Preaching mostly in the open fields, he soon learned how to capture the power of the morning air, using it as a microphone, an amplifier with his God-given voice as a speaker. Many coded messages were put to music, and the preacher would get his message across in the guise of singing.

5. The slave preacher gave a patriarchal model to a fatherless and oftentimes motherless situation. He was, in the true Pauline sense, all things to all people "that he might save some."

The slave preacher was often the connection between the slave master and the slaves, using both positions advantageously. He knew how to tell the slave master what he wanted to hear, and he knew how to tell the slave what he needed to know.

In many instances, the slave preacher was the instigator of the slave rebellions and insurrections. The slave preacher was not passive or a pun. He was respected by his parishioners and he was reckoned with by his slave master.

There are several reasons why the slave preachers were affiliated with the Baptist and Methodist persuasions. These reasons are to be understood as follows:

1. *The autonomy (self-rule) of these churches.* Especially in the Baptist tradition, there was/is no clerical hierarchy. This was/is both appealing and affirming to an oppressed people.

2. *The free-rule spirit.* Whichever way the Spirit of the Lord was leading it was all right to follow.

3. *The lack of clerical identification cards.* If one claimed he was "called" to preach, he was a preacher. Usually no questions were asked.

4. *No hierarchy of ecclesiastical sanction.* When the pastor and church agreed, it was final. No council, no synod, no association was needed to approve what the church had voted to do.

5. *Paramount respectability for the clergy.* There are historical records of slaves remaining in slavery for the emancipation of their preacher. There was a Rev. George Dupuy, (pastor of the Pleasant Green Baptist Church, Lexington, Kentucky, the oldest black Baptist church west of the Allegheny mountains, organized in 1790), who was a slave and whose members bought freedom for him and his wife while they themselves remained in slavery.

6. *Status identification which came as a result of being a member of the clerical ranks.* The black preacher has always been respected among his people.[1]

Early Black Preachers

The earliest black preachers may have preached to as many or more white congregations as they did to black congregations. This can be attributed to:

1. The fear of having a black proclaimer would give rise to

thoughts of liberation, which would bring about emancipation and would inevitably bring deterioration to the slave institution.

2. The oratorical skills and articulative talents of the black preacher made him in demand for white audiences. When the black preacher preached, something happened. Examples of this would be:

White Preacher	*Black Preacher*
Could tell the congregation Jesus was crucified between the sixth and ninth hour.	Could tell the congregation what happened *in between* the sixth and ninth hour.
What Jesus said when he died.	Could give you the discourse death and the grave had over Jesus.
Could tell you they laid Jesus in Joseph's borrowed tomb.	A telegram was sent from the tomb to the throne room in glory.
On the third appointed morning Jesus got up with all power.	Could define in a demonstrative way that power—loving power, forgiving power, I-feel-all-right power.
Jesus ascended up into the heavens.	The chief usher in glory had a special reservation for Jesus on the right hand of his Father.

The Style and Message of the Earliest Black Preachers

1. West African culture greatly influenced the hermeneutical development (that is how the gospel was made applicable to daily living), and the homiletical delivery (that is how the "story" was told).

2. Preaching was a dialogue and never a monologue. There was a call and a response. There was action and then a reaction. The preacher brought about the cause, and the Holy Spirit brought about the effect on the pews.

3. The proclaimer and those who received the proclamation were as *one*. The best of black preaching does not have an actor and an audience. There are just participants in the preaching experience.

4. The proclamation was a part of the total celebration that always had congregational participation. When this did not naturally happen, the preacher would solicit support from the congregation, which is called "praying with me."

5. The early black preacher's message had a musical tone to it. This made it "sweet" to the ears and "soothing" to the soul. What the preacher could not say, he would sing. What he could not make plain, he would put to music. What he could not tell he would tone through verbal communication.

Henry Mitchell wrote, "About the most certain statement one can make about black preaching style is that *nothing* is certain or fixed."[2]

There are some characteristics that are similar in the black preaching experience. Freedom would have to be one of the dominant characteristics found in black preaching. The black preacher has the freedom to do almost anything in the pulpit if done sincerely. "He does it his way and lets God use him."[3] This freedom leads to the colorfulness of the black worship experience. The black preacher cannot be, nor must he become, ritualized and programmed to the degree that he loses his identity of free expression from the pulpit. The black preacher must be himself before he can get into what he is saying.

> A black preacher has to let himself go. He feels what he is preaching about: freedom, sorrow, fear, rage, joy. He must make no pretense of so-called objectivity. You can't be objective when God lays His hands on you. You "preach what the Spirit says preach, and do what the Spirit says do."[4]

Much of the style of a black preacher is set by the congregation. The congregation has the freedom to actively participate in the preaching event. They are not a passive audience but one that responds to the preaching. They participate in the call and response of the sermon. This is a continuous activity throughout the worship service. The people will respond to the song and singer, the prayer and the pray-er, the sermon and the preacher.

This freedom allows the building of community between the preacher and the congregation. It sets the stage, as it were, for the communication of the Word of God to his people through his servant. This building of community is essential before there can be any communication between the preacher and the congregation. To accomplish this, black preachers incorporate personal testimony into the sermon. This freedom to be himself allows him to share himself with his congregation. This is his means of identifying with the people so he can communicate God's message.[5]

The content of the sermon must also be for both the hearer and the listener. This is true in any communication setting but appears to be more relevant in the black preaching event. "Where black preaching is to be effective, the message of the sermon must be true for both the preacher and the congregation."[6] The black congregation demands this kind of preaching. If it does not say something to me in my situation, of what real value is it? "What the black audience requires for the dialogue is both gut issue themes about survival and nourishing certainty."[7]

Another characteristic of black preaching is the slow rate of delivery. "The black preacher takes his time. When he is preaching, there is nothing more important that he could be doing."[8] This slow rate is used to gain a true comprehension of the people. The black preacher must be aware that the people need time for the message to sink in. In this slow rate of delivery, the black preacher may stammer or hesitate. This is done to build suspense and draw the congregation into the sermon.

Intonation is another characteristic of black preaching. It is the musical tone of the chant that the black preacher uses in his preaching. It is a sustained tone used in various ways to communicate to the people. "There is good reason to believe that African culture influenced all black preachers to use a musical and pleasing voice, with or without 'moaning or chanting.'"[9]

Going along with the slow rate of delivery is the use of repetition in black preaching. The black preacher will repeat his central thought or text several times throughout his sermon. This usage of repetition is done for emphasis, memory, impact and effect on the people. This use of repetition is also used in a rest and response sequence. The "experienced" black preacher learns to use repetition, rhythm, and rest to tell the story profoundly.

Another characteristic of black preaching is the use of poetic rhetoric. This gives to preaching a poetic tool to be used in building the climax of the message. O. B. Moyd defines this kind of rhetoric as "the natural fallout of faith and reason. It is honesty of the heart, mind and soul." Examples would be "white thunders were rolling, white light-ning was flashing, white winds were blowing."[10]

Dramatic Bible storytelling is another skillful tool used by the black preacher. The black preacher using good dramatics can retell an old familiar story so as to draw the people into it. It is a way to get them involved in the whole preaching event, helping them to be active participants. The black preacher uses his imagination a great deal as he draws characterizations or the retelling of a biblical story. He may add several details to enliven the story but not enough to misrepresent the real biblical story.[11] It means that the preacher becomes "spiritually involved in the story" and draws the congregation with him.[12]

This has its roots from West African religion. There the art of storytelling had been refined to communicate and carry on tribal customs and traditions. The black preacher simply picked up on this heritage and used it in his preaching style.[13]

In close connection with storytelling is role-playing. This is done by the pastor as he seeks to communicate his message. He wishes to be dramatic as he role plays. He may use pantomime or act out the parts. Again, it must be a part of his natural style in order to be effective. While he does this, it can be noted that much black preaching is done in the first person.

Along with this is the black preacher's skill in using figurative language. Pipes states, "The Negro preacher achieves his greatest stylistic success by the use of imagery or figurative language."[14]

Many of these techniques used by the black preacher are em-ployed for an emotional effect. It is believed that unless a person is emotionally affected by the preaching event, then the message has not gone as it is supposed to. "Emotions move people, while ideas which do not generate some emotion are powerless to change anybody's life."[15] The black preacher should not play on emotions merely for emotional reactions. It is done to communicate the gospel he feels compelled to proclaim. If the congregation has not been emotionally touched by the experience of worship, then nothing has happened to change their lives.

The black preacher must seek to use the language of the people when he preaches. By using such language the people can seize it and respond to it knowingly.

Another characteristic of black preaching is its Bible-centered content. The vast majority of black preaching is based upon the Bible. This Bible preaching must be life-oriented. Black congregations do not want preachers who get hung up on the "intellectual side of Christianity, theologizing and philosophying—they want to know if there is any word from the Lord. They want to know what God has told him through his encounter with the Word of God."[16]

Celebration and liberation are often two widely used themes in black preaching. The element of celebration is a vital part of the black worship experience. Christians in the black church expect it and feel that if it does not happen, all has not gone well. The preacher must celebrate to evoke celebration among his people. "Celebration in black preaching is usually emphasized near the end of the sermon or during the climax of the sermon."[17]

The liberation happens within and as a result of the celebration. Because the Lord is God, burdens are lifted; a way is made out of no way, the high is made low, and the low is made high. When the black preacher preaches, he is speaking a word of liberation to an oppressed people. That Word must lift the bowed-down heads and restore the empty souls. The best of black preaching takes place when earth is assured that heaven is still ruling and super-ruling.

THE HERMENEUTIC OF BLACK PREACHING

The biblical interpretation of hermeneutic: the chief task of hermeneutics is to convey the revelation in its contemporary context. The black preacher's proclamation must be existential in nature; he must accept the *as is* but never lose sight of the should be and could be. His message must be theologically sound. The black preacher's thoughts about who God is and what God does, must be based on a biblical foundation.

The sheep do not come Sunday after Sunday to get the pastor-preacher's opinions or thoughts. They come to hear the Word. The black preacher's message therefore must come from God, move to Christ, be led by the Holy Spirit, and find a resting place in the believer's heart.

The black preacher's message must be therapeutic and redemptive. It must speak to the here and now, as it is. The black preacher cannot afford to waste time going through theological gymnastics or exercising religious rhetoric while the masses of the people perish for the meat of the Word.

The sociologists have told us that the root of the human dilemma is social imbalance; the psychologists have told us there is a mental imbalance; the economists have told us there is a money liability versus asset imbalance—but the black preacher has to declare that there is a spiritual imbalance. Our way has attempted to overshadow God's way; our wills have been sought at the expense of doing God's will. The pastor-preacher must not tell his people that the reason they do what they do is simply because they are mischievous or they become frustrated and quarrelsome at times. The reason they do what they do and think as they think is because sin has separated them from God. The pastor-preacher must be careful that he does not overlook the root of the problem while observing the symptoms.

The Black Preacher's Message Must Convey the Truth.

> *Jesus said, "You will know the truth, and the truth will make you free" (John 8:32).*

When the truth is being presented, it does not always attract such an audience that reserved seating is needed. There will be times when the flock would rather hear a lie than the truth. They would rather be misled than go in the way of righteousness. The pastor-preacher must stand as a watchman on the wall pointing and going where the Lord says to go. He cannot be timid, afraid, or ashamed of who he is, whose he is, and why he is. He must stand sometimes as a road sign showing the way, with only the grace of God and his clear conscience as his constant companions.

The Black Preacher's Message Must Convert the Soul.

> *Your preaching task must be that of Paul: "Brethren, my heart's desire and prayer to God for Israel is, that they might be saved" (Rom. 10:1, KJV).*

Your prayer to God for the congregation over which you have been made overseer is that they might be saved. You are called upon to get up Sunday after Sunday, week after week, not merely to speak to be heard, but to preach the gospel of Jesus Christ that they might be saved.

A good indicator of your preaching effectiveness is: Is anybody being saved? Are you tickling their ears, or are you telling the everlasting story? Are they being fleeced or are they being fed?

The Black Preacher's Message Must Comfort the Disconsolate.

Jesus came to bind up the brokenhearted. As a pastor-preacher, your task is to do the same. Week after week, year after year, the flock assembles, not because they are all well and all right but because they are wounded, worn, sad, and sick. They need to know if there is a balm in Gilead, and many times they need a double portion.

The world's libraries could not contain all of the suffering and sighing, trials, and tribulations that black people have had to endure. Yet, in some mysterious way, in some unexplainable manner, they have come through floods without drowning and through fires without being consumed.

The pastor-preacher's task is to keep the light of hope glowing, to keep the footsteps determined to move forward, and to keep the eyes upon the star post in glory.

The Black Preacher's Message Must Challenge the Complacent.

Let not a man "think of himself more highly than he ought to think" (Rom. 12:3).

There are many within the congregational ranks who have concluded that "all is well in Zion." When the prophetic word is pronounced they detour it by saying, "The pastor really did tell them." The Word has ceased to be applicable to them, only significant for others.

Your task as pastor-preacher is to assure those who erroneously believe that they have time to right their wrongs. Let them know that now is the time to wake out of sleep, now is the time to be about our Father's business.

For the pastor-preacher to be an effective communicator of the

Word, he needs to understand that the gospel must be declared in the language and culture of the people. To do this you must have congregational sensitivity. Jesus was a master at this. When he was talking to lawyers, he could use the jargon of lawyers. When he was talking to tax collectors he could use their jargon; when talking to fishermen, he adapted to them. The pastor-preacher needs to know the sheep to whom he preaches if he is to speak a relevant and understandable word in their ears.

The amazing thing about God's Word is that it will fit any situation, can be explained in any language, and made pertinent in any culture.

The pastor-preacher needs to first study and learn the Word of God as it is recorded. You cannot make a correct application until you have made a correct interpretation. For example, you have to understand fully the story of Joshua fighting the battle of Jericho. Each part of the story has significance and meaning. For the pastor-preacher to retell that story in his cultural situation, he needs to make the practical application that just as God rewarded Joshua's faith and obedience and the walls fell, God rewards our faith and obedience and our walls in like manner will also fall.

The gospel must speak to the contemporary person. The question of the ages still reigns, "Is there any word from the Lord?" The pastor-preacher must give a resounding yes! Your sermonic materials must come from the living rooms of people's lives and not necessarily from the study room. You need to go down to the marketplaces, to the jailhouses, the broken homes, wherever the people gather, listen to their conversations, their hurts, their aspirations—and then speak the Word boldly and profoundly.

The wilderness is crying for a voice. What do you say to a motherless child? What do you say to a convalescent person? A chronically ill person? A person who has been unjustly wronged? You give them the good news that is found in Jesus Christ. Simply telling such persons the geography of Palestine or the missionary travels of Paul will not suffice. You, as the pastor-preacher, have to tell them about God's geography. He takes high mountains and makes them low. He takes the crooked places and makes them straight. He takes the rough places and makes them smooth. You tell them there is a way in the midst of seemingly no way. You tell them Jesus Christ is a rock in a weary land. The gospel must take a person as he is, where he is, and move him to where he ought to be, giving him the opportunity to become what he ought to be.

When Jesus met the blind man on the Jericho road, he met the man as he was. He was blind, dirty, begging, in need, a public reject, a social outcast, disinherited from the religious community, and scorned by those who passed his way. When Jesus came to him he did not say, go clean yourself up, get a shave and a haircut, get properly dressed to stand in my presence—Jesus reached out to him where he was.

As we struggle to preach the gospel of Jesus Christ, we do so with a sense of the urgency of now. We must meet people where they are, as they are, and not attempt to deal with them by how we would want them to be. There is a real danger that we may put the premium on pulpit and choir robes and not enough on being clothed in God's righteousness. Too much emphasis may get attention on padded pews and not enough praying on mercy seats.

Jesus gave grace and forgiveness so every individual might be remade in the image in which he was created. Our task can be no less. We must feed the flock with the Word of God, trusting him to give the increase and the fruit.

The sheep of the flock are spiritually hungry. There is a danger that we must guard against. Instead of giving them lunch and brunch, we must give them dinner and supper. They come for meat and too often we give them mush. They come for nourishment. We must not give them junk food. We must feed them with the Word. Preach it in season and out of season. Preach the Word!

THE BLACK CONTEXT FOR PREACHING

How can they hear without a preacher?

There are four areas I wish for us to consider in this section. They are: the herald, the homily, the hearers, and the whoop.

The Herald

"There was a man sent from God" (John 1:6).

Make special notation that the Scripture states that there was a man sent from God. Not an angel, not a saint, not seraphim or cherubim, not a celestial emissary, but a man.

I suppose one of the difficulties of the pastor's identity is realizing and accepting his own humanity. The pastor-preacher is a man. Paul said, "We have this treasure in earthen vessels, that the excellency of the power may be of God and not of us" (2 Cor. 4:7, KJV).

As men, or persons if you please, we have human limitations. If you step on our feet we flinch; if you step on our emotions we will cry, or if you step on our integrity we will retaliate. We are real people, victimized by all of the vicissitudes of real people. Once we come to grips with our humanity, we are then in a position of seeking divine wisdom and strength.

The pastor-preacher must never think or conclude that he is the power station locked up within himself. He must decrease while the Christ he proclaims increases. I have heard too many pastor-preachers declare brazenly after the Lord had used them to preach his Word, "I really did it, I slew them today!" The truth of the matter is the Lord, in his divine will and goodness, decided to use us in spite of us to do his work. We cannot boast of what we have done. We can only praise God for what he has permitted us to do.

It is interesting to note that when the Eternal God chooses to speak to finite man, he uses a person to speak to persons. He does not have to, but he decides to do it that way. No doubt the Lord of life could put his message out on the morning air or speak it softly in the hearts of men, and yet when he chooses to speak he gets persons of mortal, sinful flesh to speak everlasting and righteous truths.

The personhood of the pastor-preacher has to be affirmed both to himself and to the congregation he strives to serve. The pastor-preacher has to realize that he is not a one-man band, nor should he attempt to be one. He ought to see himself as the conductor of the orchestra. That way he can be assured of a much better sound. There are still a few congregations around that expect the pastor-preacher, and even require him to be it all, to do it all and know it all. This is unreal and unbiblical. The Holy Spirit has given various gifts to different members of the congregation for the edifying of the body of Christ. For the pastor-preacher to conclude that he will do all of the preaching—all of the teaching, all of the administration, all of the visitation, all of the music ministry, all of the counseling, and all of whatever needs to be done—is tragic to pastoral ministry effectiveness. The pastor-preacher is human and he speaks a divine message through a human channel. He speaks that message to human beings of like passions and persuasions as himself, and he is convicted and comforted by the same gospel that he proclaims.

Sent from God. What then separates or sets the pastor-preacher apart from others? Is he just another one of the fellows? Yes and no. He is human with all the human limitations, and yet the Scripture states that there was a man sent from God. This being sent from God is most significant. It gives the pastor-preacher divine authorization. He preaches not his word, nor does he come in his own power or wisdom; but as one sent from God, he has heaven's approval on that which he has been sent to do. When the pastor-preacher proclaims God's Word, he has the assurance that that Word will not go out void but will accomplish the purpose for which God has sent it.

The calling and being sent from God gives the pastor-preacher the divine authorization to proclaim God's Word boldly, to rebuke and correct ungodly behavior, to teach the commands of Christ unapologetically, and the permission to stand in the congregation as the Lord's representative. When I reflect over my pastor-preacher accountability to God who called and sent me and then consider the awesome responsibility to the congregation over which the Holy Spirit has made me overseer, I am honored and humbled. Honored because the Lord would use me and yet humbled because I am profoundly aware of my unworthiness for the task.

The herald, pastor-preacher, must hear the Word from the Lord and then deliver that Word to the people. His task is to assure the people—there is a word from the Lord.

The Homily

"How shall they preach, except they be sent?" (Rom. 10:15, KJV).

The question to consider is: How shall we preach?

For the pastor-preacher to declare the Word with clarity and boldness, he should be aware of four basic sermon preparation factors.

The first would be the *biblical text*. Your sermonic material should for the most part be based upon and derived from the Bible. There is no substitute for the Bible text. I am sure you have heard, as I have, many sermons with a hundred quotations from various authors and scholars but very few quotes from the Bible. If you want to quote someone when you are preaching quote Jesus. If you want to quote a reference work use the Bible. You will not go wrong!

The text should be prayerfully read and reread so as much understanding as possible can be gathered directly from the text. You should be aware to read the text as it is written and not attempt to reread the text and twist it to say what you want it to say.

In properly dealing with the text you should do a word study of all key words, paying special attention to what you may consider little words. The use of a Bible dictionary, biblical encyclopedia, lexicon, or word-study aids can help you in your preparation.

An exegetical study can then be done of the text. The word *exegesis* means to take out of the Scripture text. An exegetical study is taking all of the words and thoughts and putting them together coming to a conclusion of what the Bible text is saying. The opposite of exegesis (taking out) is *eisegesis* (reading into the Scriptures). The latter is most dangerous in sermon preparation and in just reading the Scriptures. There is a tendency to want the Bible to say what we want it to say rather than letting it speak to us as it is written.

After the text has been adequately dealt with, you are then ready to move into the second area of sermon preparation, and that is the *context*. The context is the historicity or the background of the text. In the context you are seeking to understand the historical root of the text. The kinds of questions you will want to answer in considering the text within the context are: Who wrote the text? Why was it written? To whom was it written? What is the possible time of writing? What were the conditions or circumstances at the time that made for the writing? What was the intention of the writer as best we can tell? There is a temptation to take the text completely out of context. When this is done you can end up with a false text. Good biblical preaching comes from good Bible study. There can be no substitute for doing our preparation. If we are going to speak for God we must use God's Word. Nothing else will do.

The *subject* is the third factor in sermon preparation. The subject should come from either the text or the context. If not directly, it ought to at least be shown how the subject you are using can be correlated and fitted into the text. The subject and the text should be as one. I have heard many sermons that have had good texts but that is about the only positive thing I could say about the message. Flowery subjects ("Puppy Love That Ended Up in the Dog House") and passion-arousing titles ("It Feels Too Good to Quit") may attract people's attention to arcades on the side roads, but when people come to hear the word of the Lord, they want it pure, profound, and personally directed.

The fourth factor is *sermon delivery*. There are several styles of sermon delivery, and you will have to use the styles that are fitting to your abilities. I wish to list these styles showing the advantages and disadvantages of each.

A. Verbatim Manuscript
  1. Advantages: you have to write down your thoughts completely beforehand. This gives you an opportunity to recall all of your research and preparation without the possibility of forgetting something you intended to say. The verbatim manuscript helps keep your previous thoughts before you no matter how distracting the present situation may be.
  2. Disadvantages: you are locked in permaturely sometimes as to what you are going to say. What you intended to say may not be what needs to be said at the actual moment of preaching. You may receive additional inspiration or thoughts on something you had not previously considered.

B. The Outline Format
  1. Advantages: your research and thoughts can be systematically arranged, giving you an outline or a structure to follow in your delivery. This method also allows you the opportunity of flexibility because you can insert a new thought without completely changing all that you had previously intended to say.
  2. Disadvantages: your prior ordering or structuring may not be the most feasible at the particular time of preaching. You may become overly locked in believing you have to stay with what you have prepared.

C. Extemporaneous or Free Preaching
  1. Advantages: this type of sermon delivery is not to be confused

with unprepared preaching or simply preaching at random, saying whatever comes into our minds and out of our mouths. Your sermon preparation can be done in advance allowing you the opportunity to internalize and personalize the message until the Word becomes incarnated in you. You have freedom within structure. You know what you are going to say, and you can adapt it to fit the situation.

2. Disadvantages: this type of preaching if not done correctly can cause you to travel all over the Bible, say a whole lot about everything, and speak specifically to no issue or thought. Another disadvantage is you may preach impulsively without preaching with information or inspiration. You have to be careful not to say just what comes to mind.

D. Storytelling

The preacher of the gospel has been called to tell the greatest story of all times—Jesus is Christ, both Lord and Savior. Those who preach ought to be able to tell the story well.

1. Advantages: when preaching a Bible story, all of the information and materials needed to tell the story is given in the Bible text. The preacher will at various points use his imagination (within the boundary of biblical theology) to bring the story to life. The story has to be told in the vernacular or language of the people. This enables the preacher using this sermon style to talk the language of the hearers. Another advantage of storytelling is that the preacher and the hearers should be able to secure a point of contact within the story. This is necessary to put the proclaimer and the pew within the story.

2. Disadvantages: the preacher and hearers can get so caught up in the story as story that the theme and lesson may be missed. The story may be erroneously told, thereby changing the whole meaning and significance of the story. Correlation may not take place between the biblical story and the contemporary situation.

E. Dramatic Monologue

In this sermonic style the preacher "acts" out the biblical story or the sermon theme.

1. Advantages: the word can become flesh through the preacher. The congregation participates in the sermon by becoming a part of the drama. The preacher has freedom and flexibility to be creative in his delivery and freedom of physical movement. The congregation receives the sermon as action and adventure. They become the channel through which the sermon comes.
2. Disadvantages: the preacher can loose his identity of being a preacher and attempt to become an actor. The congregation can sit back at a distance and conclude that they are only watching a drama. Too much flexibility in sermonic materials can lead to a preaching failure. You may have given a good performance but no preaching.

The pastor-preacher will have to choose a style or styles that are suitable to his personality, his abilities, and his creativity. I would suggest that the pastor-preacher do what is best for him, being flexible in delivery but firm in preaching one Lord, one faith, and one baptism.

The Hearers

"How shall they hear?" (Rom. 10:14, KJV).

The pastor-preacher should always keep his preaching objective clear: to reach people with the gospel of Jesus Christ. Our preaching task is not to write homilies, deliver profound discourses, to present theological arguments, or to expose our training or lack of it. Our task as preachers is to speak just one word that will reach, touch, and find a resting place in the believer's heart. The sheep who gather Sunday after Sunday, week after week, do so not to hear us but to hear the Word of the Lord. We, as we are, have no message, no story, and no power. The excellency of the power of proclamation is of God and not of ourselves.

It matters not how much preaching we have done. The real question is how much hearing has taken place?

There are several factors both on the preacher's part and on the hearers' part that hinder or prevent hearing. Let us first consider what prevents hearing on the hearers' part.

The refusal to hear will hinder or prevent hearing. Everyone who assembles in the house of the Lord does not do so to hear the Word of the Lord. They come for many reasons. Some come to see and be seen, to find out the latest gossip and give the latest in exchange. Some come because of ritualistic conditioning. They have always come to this particular place, at this particular time to do this particular thing. It matters not who or what is before them, what is being said or not said. They did not come to hear the Word preached, and they are not going to disappoint themselves by changing their agenda.

The refusal to hear the Word is serious because the Scriptures teach us that they will never be saved unless they hear the Word. They will never hear the Word without a preacher. This refusal to hear is rooted in sin with branches of disobedience and rebellion. Those who assemble themselves in the house of the Lord with a refusal attitude will not hear the Word no matter who preaches, or how it is preached. You as a pastor-preacher need to be keenly aware of those in the flock who have this disposition. If you are not aware of this for what it is, you can develop a complex thinking there is something personally wrong with you or with your preaching ability. You can rest assured that those who refuse to hear the Word are not rejecting you; they are rejecting the Lord Almighty.

Lack of biblical understanding can and does hinder hearing. The Word of God has the power within it to transform and convert the most ignorant person. The Scriptures teach us that God's Word will not return unto him void but will accomplish that to which he has sent it. This is why it is crucial that the pastor-preacher preaches the Word. Our philosophies, our theologies, our opinions, our interpretations are not adequate or sufficient to rebuke ignorance and stubbornness. Only the Word of God, preached unashamedly, can do that.

Many times when the biblical word is being preached, the hearers will take odds with it because they are ignorant of what the Bible really states. If something is being presented that they have not heard before or has not been stressed to them, they will take odds or become indifferent to that particular thought. A good preaching ministry should be backed up with a good teaching ministry. If the cliché is true, "People are usually down on what they are not up on," then the pastor-preacher had better make sure that the flock is up on the Word of God.

The personality or style of the preacher can oftentimes hinder hearing. Paul was profoundly aware of this, and that is why he said he would become all things to all men that he might save some. The pastor-preacher should be aware that his personality, including his mannerisms, his tone of voice, his delivery style, his pulpit garments, his vocabulary, his physical presence in the pulpit are vitally important to the hearing level of the congregation. Sometimes the congregation cannot hear what you are saying for listening to what you are doing. Pray that you will do nothing that will hinder the effectiveness of the proclamation of the gospel.

Bad reception hinders hearing. If your vocabulary, usage of words, sentence structures, pronunciation, diction, and delivery are foreign or unacceptable to the congregation, you are the one who has to adapt to them. I have known preachers who refused to talk the language of the people when they were preaching. They didn't preach too long to those congregations.

The physical hearing of the congregation can be impaired by the hearer not being able to hear what you are saying. You may have one of the greatest sermons, but what good is it if no one can hear you? The public address system, the pulpit, and congregation's seating arrangement should all be conducive to hearing the Word.

The congregation's lack of involvement in the preaching experience can be a hindrance to hearing. Preaching is a dialogue and not a monologue. The congregation should never feel or think that they have come to watch you perform for them. The preacher and those who are preached to must become as one, mutually sharing in the preaching experience.

Satan hinders hearing. Evil and the forces of evil are real and have to be reckoned with as such. There will be situations that will develop, seemingly right at the time of preaching, which will attempt to be the source of major distraction from the hearing of the Word. The pastor-preacher needs to be aware of these and deal with them adequately.

The lack of biblical understanding, the refusal to hear the Word, bad reception, Satan and the forces of evil, lack of involvement in the preaching experience all can be deterrents in the hearing of the Word. These factors usually develop on the hearer's side. Now let us consider a few factors on the preacher's side that can hinder hearing.

The pastor-preacher can hinder hearing by his lack of sermon preparation. Charles Spurgeon said of the preacher, "If you are going to speak, say something." I agree. How many times have you heard the preacher who had nothing to say and who was saying nothing keep asking the hearers "to pray with him" or "say amen." I believe that most of the praying should take place before the sermon, and the gospel preached true and bold will invoke its own amens. We as pastor-preachers often look at the hearers and wonder why they are not going along with us or wonder why we receive such a cold reception while we are preaching. I wonder if we are not partially responsible in that we have not adequately prepared ourselves for the task before us?

Lack of enthusiasm on the preacher's part hinders hearing. If you get up to preach and do so as if you wish you were somewhere else, it will reciprocate to the hearers. They will wish they were someplace else. If you are dry, dull, and dead in your delivery, do not expect an overzealous and enthusiastic response from the hearers. If you come as the "doctor," and you are not overly excited about the "medicine," why should the "patients" (congregation) be so. You must do as the old slave preacher Jasper Jones remarked when asked how he preached the way he did. He said, "I read myself full, think myself clear, pray myself hot, and then I let myself go." Certainly this is good advice for the pastor-preacher to duplicate in his sermon preparation.

Not having congregational sensitivity can hinder hearing. The pastor-preacher should know his sheep. Where they hurt, have burdens, anxieties, frustrations, and doubts is where your preaching ought to be centered. Preaching in generalities and answering questions no one has asked will not be sufficient in feeding the flock. The pastor-preacher has to understand as best he can where his people are coming from in their day by day experiences. We must preach to specific issues and address particular situations. When Jesus was confronted by a lawyer he spoke in a language understandable by the lawyer, and he addressed himself to the particular issue. When Jesus spoke to fishermen, he used their language and spoke to their situation. To be an effective communicator of the gospel, we must learn this early in our preaching ministry and continually be reminded of it.

Repetitive and ritual preaching can be a hindrance to hearing. In pastoral preaching, the pastor-preacher is the same person preaching to the same congregation week after week, year after year. It is very easy to get locked into a particular mode or style of preaching and use it on a continual basis. When you are preaching in the same preaching context you need to be flexible and innovative in sermon style, delivery, rhythm, and approach. The congregation should not know where you are going to park every time you pull up. You should come with a fresh and vital word each time you stand at the sacred desk proclaiming God's Word. There are some pastor-preachers who believe they have to put Jesus on the cross, lay him in Joseph's tomb, and have him get up "early" Sunday morning each time they preach.

The pastor-preacher's use or misuse of the preaching opportunity can be a hindrance to hearing. The pastor-preacher should be cautious that he does not use the preaching opportunity or the sacred place of the pulpit as a whipping board or as a retaliatory post to get back at the congregation in general or any individual in particular. The preaching opportunity is not a time to degenerate but rather to regenerate, not to "cuss" them out but to convert them within. Only the gospel preached out of a loving heart with power given from the Holy Spirit can convince, convey, convict, and convert those who hear the Word.

The pastor-preacher has to be sensitive to the many factors which hinder the hearing ability of the congregation. The nonreadiness of the congregation, the unpreparedness of the preacher, the refusal on the part of the congregation to hear the Word, and the refusal on the pastor-preacher's part to preach the Word with bold enthusiasm—all serve to deafen the ear of those who hear the gospel of Jesus Christ. The gospel is too important not to be heard. Let us pray that the Lord will open our mouths to preach and open the ears of the flock that they might hear.

The Whoop

> Even things without life giving sound, whether pipe or harp, except they give a distinction in the sounds, how shall it be known what is piped or harped? For if the trumpet give an uncertain sound, who shall prepare himself to the battle?
> So likewise ye, except ye utter by the tongue words easy to be understood, how shall it be known what is spoken? for ye shall speak into the air (1 Cor. 14:7-9, KJV).

In this final section of the pastor as preacher, I want to discuss what is considered the zenith or apex of the best of black preaching: the "whoop."

There is no operational definition for the whoop (at least I know of none). There are distinctive qualities and peculiar characteristics that help identify the whoop as such.

Within the black preaching tradition there is a general call and response, dialogue-type approach in the preaching experience. The black preacher in his sermon delivery usually starts slowly, speaking each word on its own and sort of lazily moves to the next word or thought. As he does this the congregation sits in anticipation "praying" with him as he builds momentum and arouses anxious enthusiasm in what he is next going to say. As the black preacher moves from thought to thought and builds sentence upon sentence, he begins in a deliberate, rhythmic manner to move the congregation along the same line he is going, seeking to move them toward the same level of anticipation and celebration. As he moves toward home—the end of the message—all of what he has previously spoken is brought to bear upon one particular moment. If he has raised a question throughout his sermon, if he has seemed confused or bewildered by the events of the story he has just told, all are answered in the whoop. It is in the whoop that the prodigal son comes home. It is in the whoop that the woman who met Jesus at the well goes home. It is in the whoop that Jesus dies on the cross and arises on the third appointed morning. The whoop makes the wandering in the wilderness worthwhile. The whoop makes understanding out of misunderstanding, joy out of sorrow, and hope out of despair.

Distinction in the Sound. The apostle Paul writes that even instruments have to give a clear distinct sound if we are to understand and appreciate the music they make.

There is a radical difference between whooping and hollering. Loud preaching with shuts and cries, moaning and groaning at the end is not whooping; that is hollering. When you have told the story with boldness and the Holy Spirit has come within his preacher and among his people, then you can whoop. In fact, good preaching, like a good piece of meat, will make its own gravy. You have no business whooping or attempting to whoop if you have not preached. A word of caution should be given to the pastor-preacher who puts too much emphasis on how he is going to close the sermon rather than on what he is going to say during the message.

Hollering takes place when the pastor-preacher has erroneously calculated that the Holy Spirit and the people are at one with him. He believes that he has a pleasant voice, a singing tone or moan to his words, and he believes he has had enough experience in preaching to do just about whatever he chooses. The pastor-preacher who does this has built his climax but forgotten to lay the foundation and the supporting walls to hold the message. An example would be a person making the best icing in town for the worst cake in town. A well-prepared cake with all of the right ingredients will make its own icing. In fact, it may taste better without the icing.

If you as a pastor-preacher have the gift of voice fluctuation or have a soothing, singing tone to your speech, you may, with the Holy Spirit's permission whoop. If you do not naturally have it, you do not need it to be the best preacher God can have. If you will merely look and listen around you, some of the world's greatest preachers were not and are not "whoopers." The one factor they all have in common is that they can tell the story. You should be challenged because you, through the grace of God, can tell that same story.

How Not to Just Speak in the Air. The way to be sure that your whooping is not just hollering, that your preaching is not just a play on words signifying nothing, is to make sure your sermon is biblically based, Christ-centered, Holy-Spirit-led, and people-directed. If you will do this, you will be doing that for which you were called.

You should spend as much time preparing *yourself* as you do preparing the sermon. For the preached Word of God to be effective, it has to be God's Word as given in the Bible, and to live it has to become personalized and incarnated in the preacher.

Know what you are going to preach and then be bold and enthusiastic in preaching it. There is shame and disgrace when the preacher gets up to preach and gives the impression that he wants to apologize for being a preacher or for what he is about to say. God's Word needs no apology, and God's preacher need not make any excuses for who he is or whose he is.

Keep your body under subjection both before and after you have preached. If you are preaching eternal truths but are living present lies, if you are pointing to the way called straight but you are going the way of the crooked, how effective will your preaching be? The sermon happens as much in the public as it does in the pulpit.

Trust the Lord who has called you to preach his word that he will supply your every need. You are not your own, doing your own ministry, speaking your own words. You have been called of him to speak for him. He will not fail you. The Lord sent ravens to feed Elijah by the brook of Cherith even in the midst of a drought. He gives the sparrow enough straw to build his house. What more will he do for those who trust him and walk upright before him?

Finally, my brethren, be strong in the Lord, in the power of his might. Preach the Word!

3

The Pastor as Teacher

Philip ran to him, and heard him reading Isaiah the prophet, and asked, "Do you understand what you are reading?" And he said, "How can I, unless someone guides me?"
And he invited Philip to come up and sit with him (Acts 8:30-31).

The question Philip asked the Ethiopian eunuch is the question the pastor-teacher must ask the flock: "Do you understand what you are reading?" The answer of the flock is also the same, "How can [we], unless someone guides [us]?" That someone who is to guide the flock in biblical understanding is the pastor-teacher.

For black people the pastor has been referred to as "doctor" or "doc," and it has been meant in a real way. He was and is considered the doctor, not because of his academic accomplishment but because of his unique teaching techniques. The black pastor has had that rare ability to take the incomprehensible and make it understandable. He can take the complex and simplify it. The black pastor's schooling has come primarily from the "living room of life" and not necessarily from the classroom of higher learning.

To get a clearer understanding of the pastor-teacher, let us consider Jesus.

JESUS ON TEACHING

In the New Testament we find numerous titles used to describe the person and work of Jesus. The total number of titles used is well over forty.[1] Within certain circles some titles tend to be more emphasized than others, and frequently the choice of titles given to Jesus reveals a great deal about the views of that particular circle. One group may emphasize that Jesus was (is) the "Prophet"; another the "Savior"; another "Lord"; another the "Messiah." Within the four Gospels one of the titles most frequently used to describe Jesus is "Teacher." This title is used of Jesus some forty-five times.

It is the unanimous witness of the gospel tradition and reaction that one of the prominent functions of Jesus during his public ministry was teaching (Matt. 4:23, The Marcan parallel in 1:39 uses the word *preaching*.) and that despite his lack of formal training (Mark 6:2-3; John 7:15), he was correctly recognized as a teacher or "rabbi" (Mark 12:14; John 3:2). Although Jesus had gone through the normal pre-scribed course of instruction, his wisdom and manner of teaching resembled that of the other rabbis, so that it was not unnatural to ascribe this title to him.[2] Like other rabbis, Jesus proclaimed the divine law (Mark 12:28-34), taught in the synagogues (Mark 1:21-28,39; 3:1-6; 6:1-6), gathered disciples (Mark 1:16-20; 3:13-19; see John 1:35-51; 1 Cor. 15:5), debated with the scribes (Mark 7:5; 11:27-33; 12:13-17), was asked to settle legal disputes (Mark 12:13-17; Luke 12:13-15), sat as he taught (Mark 4:1; Mark 9:35; Matt. 5:1; Luke 4:20), supported his teaching with Scripture (Mark 2:25-26; 4:12, 10:6-8,19; Matt. 12:40; 18:16), used poetic-didactic techniques to help his disciples memorize.[3]

There were also differences between Jesus and the rabbis in how he taught, for Jesus often taught in the open fields and countryside as well as in the synagogues (Mark 4:1; 6:32-44; 8:1-9; Mark 2:13; Matt. 5:1); and his association with women, tax collectors, sinners, and children (Mark 2:14-17; 10:13-16; Matt. 11:16-19; Luke 7:39; 15:1-2) was quite "unrabbinic." The relationship between Jesus and his disciples also differed from that between the rabbis and their disciples. Normally a pupil was a disciple of the tradition of his teacher, but the disciples of Jesus were exactly that: disciples of Jesus. Their message was not just the words of Jesus, although they did "receive" and thus now "delivered" his words; but the message consisted of the person of their teacher as well.[4]

THE FORM OF JESUS' TEACHING

Jesus was an outstanding teacher. Without the use of modern-day audio-visual materials and props, he captured the attention of his audience. This ability of Jesus at times even created problems for him. According to Mark 4:1, on one occasion Jesus attracted such a crowd by his teaching that he had to enter a boat on the Sea of Galilee and teach from it. The miracle of the feeding of the five thousand recorded in Mark 6:30-44 was due in part to the fact that the crowd simply forgot about their need for food because of their fascination and interest in the teaching of Jesus (see vv. 35-36). In the above examples it should be noted that the crowds are portrayed as gathering not because of any miracles Jesus was performing, for none are mentioned, but because of their interest in the teaching of Jesus.

Why was Jesus such a fascinating teacher? What caused these large crowds to follow him? In reply one might say that it was *what* Jesus said that drew the crowds. With Jesus the voice of prophecy had once again returned to Israel after four hundred years. One reason people came to hear Jesus was that many were convinced that God was speaking through Jesus of Nazareth, and that what he was saying was indeed the word of God. (Luke 5:1; 11:28; Mark 4:14-20). Yet every Christian teacher and preacher must confess that at times he has proclaimed the same *what*, the same word of God, that Jesus taught and has been less than exciting. There must therefore be other factors which together with the *what* made Jesus the exciting teacher that he was.

No doubt an additional factor that enters the picture involves the personality of Jesus, for the personality of Jesus gave life and vitality to his message. People loved to listen to Jesus because of the kind of person he was. Publicans, sinners, children, the crowds—all found in Jesus one in whom they enjoyed being near. It was therefore not only *what* he taught, but also *who* he was that attracted people to hear him. Closely related to this was the authority with which Jesus taught (see Mark 1:21-28). Jesus' message, unlike that of the scribes and the rabbis, did possess a derivative authority from the rabbis of the past but possessed an immediate authority (Matt. 5:21-22,27-28,31-32,33-35, 38-39,43-45), and it should be noted that the message of Jesus was frequently accompanied by signs and wonders (Mark 1:22,27,39; 3:10-11; see John 3:2).

There is still another factor that made Jesus a great teacher which is frequently overlooked. This is the *how*, or the exciting manner in which Jesus taught.

Let us now consider some of the methods Jesus used in his teaching.

Overstatement.[5] One means by which Jesus sought to capture the attention of his listeners was in overstating a truth in such a way that the resulting exaggeration forcefully brought home the point he was attempting to make. Such overstatement is a characteristic of Semitic speech, and we possess numerous examples of this in the Gospels. In Luke 14:26, Jesus says, "If anyone comes to me and does not hate his own father and mother and wife and children and brothers and sisters, yes, and even his own life, he cannot be my disciple."

Jesus is using overstatement to make his point. The point he is making is that even natural affection for our loved ones dare not interfere or take precedence over loyalty to him. Most times love and loyalty for Jesus and love and loyalty for parents go hand in hand, but when a choice must be made natural affections must be set aside out of love for Jesus.

Hyperbole.[6] Closely related to Jesus' use of overstatement is his use of hyperbole, for both have in common the use of exaggeration. The two can be distinguished by the degree of exaggeration. In overstatement, the saying could be understood and physically possible to carry out. Thus if you were to interpret Jesus literally you could cut off your hand or pluck out your eye. In hyperbole, the gross exaggeration makes such a literal fulfillment or portrayal impossible. An example would be Matthew 23:23-24. "Woe to you, scribes and Pharisees, hypocrites! for you tithe mint and dill and cummin, and have neglected the weightier matters of the law, justice and mercy and faith; these you ought to have done, without neglecting the others. You blind guides, straining out a gnat and swallowing a camel!" The degree of exaggeration can be seen in that it would be humanly impossible for one to literally swallow a camel.

Pun. Another form Jesus used in his teaching was the pun. A pun is a play on words in which either homonyms (like-sounding words) suggest two or more different meanings, or the same word may have two different meanings. An example would be Luke 9:59-60: "To another he said, 'Follow me.' But he said, 'Lord, let me first go and bury my father.' But he said to him, 'Leave the dead to bury their own dead.'" In this difficult saying the same word *dead* is used with a double meaning and means, "Let the spiritually dead bury their own physically dead."

   Simile.[7] A simile is an explicit comparison between two things that are essentially unlike each other and that are introduced by a connective such as "like," "as," or "than" or by a verb such as "seems." Some examples of simile are:

> Behold, I send you out as sheep in the midst of wolves; so be wise as serpents and innocent as doves (Matt. 10:16).
> For as Jonah was three days and three nights in the belly of the whale, so will the Son of man be three days and three nights in the heart of the earth (Matt. 12:40).
> If you had faith as a grain of mustard seed, you could say to this sycamine tree, "Be rooted up, and be planted in the sea," and it would obey you (Luke 17:6).

   In the above examples the elements of comparison and dissimilarity are quite clear. The believer is likened to sheep and told to be like serpents in wisdom and doves in their blamelessness, whereas the unbelievers are likened to wolves. Jesus' resurrection is likened to Jonah's stay in the belly of the fish. The believers faith is likened to a seed.

   Metaphor.[8] A metaphor, like a simile, is a comparison between two essentially unlike things. In contrast to a simile, however, where an explicit comparison is made (The eye is like a lamp for the body.), the metaphor makes an implicit comparison ("The eye is the lamp of the body" Matt. 6:22.). The Gospels contain numerous examples of such figures of speech, for Jesus was fond of using analogies. The following are some examples of metaphors in the Gospels:

> Take heed, beware of the leaven of the Pharisees and the leaven of Herod (Mark 8:15).
> You are the salt of the earth; but if the salt has lost its taste, how shall its saltness be restored? (Matt. 5:13; see Mark 9:49-50).
> The harvest is plentiful, but the laborers are few; pray therefore the Lord of the harvest to send out laborers into his harvest (Matt. 9:37-38)

   Although they are things essentially alike, Jesus compares the teaching (Matt. 16:12) and the hypocrisy (Luke 12:1) of the Pharisees to leaven or sourdough. In the other examples, Jesus likens his followers to salt and the light of the world; the masses who follow him to a harvest.

Another type of metaphor found in the Gospels is the familiar "I am" sayings found in the Gospel of John.[9] Some of these are:

> I am the bread of life; he who comes to me shall not hunger, and he who believes in me shall never thirst (John 6:35).
> I am the light of the world; he who follows me will not walk in darkness, but will have the light of life (John 8:12).
> I am the vine, you are the branches. He who abides in me, and I in him, he it is that bears much fruit, for apart from me you can do nothing (John 15:5).

Jesus also used proverbs as a teaching method.[10] These no doubt stand in the wisdom tradition of the Middle East. Examples would be:

> Where your treasure is, there will your heart be also (Matt. 6:21).
> All who take the sword will perish by the sword (Matt. 26:52).
> If a kingdom is divided against itself, that kingdom cannot stand (Mark 3:24).

The riddle was used by Jesus. With the riddle the individual is challenged to discover the concealed meaning. Examples:

> I will destroy this temple that is made with hands, and in three days I will build another, not made with hands (Mark 14:58).
> From the days of John the Baptist until now the kingdom of heaven has suffered violence, and men of violence take it by force (Matt. 11:12).

He who had wisdom or would be wise was admonished to hear these words and understand them, not logically but spiritually.

Jesus used paradox to bring out the true meaning of a thought. The paradox would be a statement that may appear to be self-contradictory or at odds with common sense, but when fully examined and explained it contains much truth.

Examples are Jesus' sayings that he who would be greatest must be servant of all (Matt. 23:11); he who would be first must be a slave of all (Mark 9:35); a grain of wheat must die before life will come forth (John

12:24); it is not what goes into the mouth that defiles a person, it is what comes out (Matt. 15:17-19).

Jesus used irony. Irony can refer to an event or result that is opposite to what one would normally expect. Jesus explaining who is your neighbor in the parable of the good Samaritan would be a good example. You would have expected the religious and devout leaders of Israel, the Levite and the priest, to have rendered assistance to the wounded man. Instead the Samaritan, a half-breed—so far as Israel was concerned—defiled and degrading, was the one who gave assistance.

Jesus asked questions to arouse and awaken the awareness of the people. One of the sure ways of getting them to understand who he was and what he was about was to ask questions concerning his ministry.

An example would be the healing of a man on the sabbath day. Jesus asked, "Is it lawful on the sabbath to do good or to do harm, to save life or to kill?" (Mark 3:1-4).

Jesus was diverse in his teaching methodologies. He used many approaches, adjusting them to fit the ears of his audience. Our techniques in the teaching ministry should be equally as diverse and adaptable to the congregational level of understanding.

PASTORAL TEACHING

Seeing the multitudes, he went up into a mountain: and when he was set, his disciples came unto him: And he opened his mouth and taught them (Matt. 5:1-2, KJV).

Seeing the Multitudes

The first task of the pastor-teacher is to see the multitudes. He must have congregational sensitivity and pastoral sense to know the needs of the flock that the Holy Spirit has made him overseer.

Jesus confronted Peter with the pastoral mandate: if you love me, feed my sheep. This is the assignment of the pastor-teacher: feed the sheep.

In order for the pastor to see the multitudes he must be at a different level and view the congregation from a different perspective.

You will never "see" the multitudes until you have first "seen" yourself. You must equip and prepare yourself before you can teach (feed) the flock.

I suppose one of the reasons there is so little Christian education fervor in black churches is because of the low educational level of the black clergy. There was a time when the black pastor was *the* educated man in the congregation and in the community. Just look around you, my brother, and you will discover that day has come and gone. This is an age of educational specialists. Your task as a pastor-teacher is to be a biblically-oriented teaching specialist. You should never apologize for the Bible, and you should never applaud your ignorance of not knowing it.

You will have to prepare yourself for the task of feeding the flock. You should take advantage of every teaching opportunity that you may be thoroughly equipped, rightly dividing the word of truth.

This will involve enrolling in "school." This school may be an accredited college or university, a Bible college, seminary, religious institute, Christian education workshops, seminars, state associations or district conferences, or just the weekly fellowship of pastors coming together to study and share God's Word.

You will need to subscribe to religious journals and magazines to keep abreast of the ever changing sociological and theological trends.

You should discipline yourself to have a regular reading schedule and accumulate books, articles, and materials that can be developed into a library. One of the things Paul requested of Timothy to bring him to Rome was his books (2 Tim. 4:13). Even though his physical body was imprisoned and confined, he did not want his mind to be imprisoned.

To see the multitudes you will need sensitivity. Jesus had so much sensitivity to the people that he wept over them, for he saw them as sheep not having a shepherd. We, as pastors-teachers, need to do some "weeping," not in pity, but weep until we begin to prepare and plan and lead the flock into biblically taught pastures.

There are needs, hurts, and aspirations of the flock that the pastor has to be tuned in to. The people's desire is to get to the Promised Land, but they do not know how to get there. The pastor-teacher's task is to feed them with spiritual nourishment and nurture them with the Word of God so they can make the journey successfully.

To have sensitivity you will have to sit where they sit for a little while. You must not conclude that your people are farther down the road of biblical understanding than they really are. It is with regret that I write this, but with a sense of necessity I must say it. Most good Christian people are biblically illiterate. What I mean is, they believe in the Bible as God's Word, but are profoundly ignorant of what the Bible teaches. You, brother pastor, will have to, for the most part, combat ignorance with information, apathy with awareness, and complacency with confrontation.

It is one thing to see the multitudes and withdraw. That is avoidance. It is something else to see the multitudes and draw near. That is shepherding. To draw near you will need a sincere desire to help the multitude. Your Christian education attitude must be over, above, and beyond your flock if you are to feed and guide them, but your pastoral attitude must be with and among them if they are going to follow your lead. The sheep will respond to the shepherd when they realize he has a sincere desire to help them. By the mere nature of sheep they will respond to a shepherd's voice. That voice must be spoken in sincerity and honesty.

We are in a position of feeding the multitude when we as pastors-teachers can move toward the flock where they are, as they are, and begin through the grace of the Lord to move them where they should be.

Jesus saw the multitudes because he was at a different level. He understood his personhood of being the Bread of life. His sensitivity was with the people as he moved with compassion because of them, and he had a sincere desire to help them.

When the pastor-teacher has developed to this point, he is on the way to being obedient to the Lord's command: feed my sheep.

Getting Set

The second task of the pastor-teacher is getting set. Jesus did not teach until he was set. The pastor-teacher cannot teach until he is set.

To get set, the pastor-teacher has to be taught himself. You are in no position to give out what you have not taken in. You must be taught the Word and be dedicated to being a student of the Word. The members of the flock are sheep looking to the pastor as shepherd to feed them with the Word of God. To lead the congregation into the rich pasture of biblical understanding, the pastor-teacher has to go ahead of the flock in preparing himself for the challenge.

Your biblical understanding or lack of it will influence the effectiveness of the Christian education programs you present to the flock. If you have enthusiasm and zeal for the didactic (teaching) ministry, it will be contagious, causing others to want to study and learn as you have done. You should always see yourself in the role of a servant sharing the Word with God's sheep. You are not the ultimate authority with all earthly and heavenly answers. This approach of humbly sharing and presenting the eternal truths of the Bible will greatly enhance the seeking and study habits of the congregation.

To get set, the pastor-teacher needs to determine what he is going to teach. Jesus did not begin his teaching ministry haphazardly or at random with no perspective of direction and no purpose or goal. He knew who he was, why he was, what he was about, and how he was going to accomplish the task before him. Jesus even knew the opposition he was going to encounter as a consequence of his teaching. The pastor-teacher cannot afford to be less purpose oriented.

As the pastor-teacher you should have a plan and a procedure to your teaching ministry. To do this you first need to analyze and evaluate as best you can the Christian education level of the congregation. You should be cautious in this area, not to assume that your members are farther up the ladder than they really are.

Flexibility and adaptability will have to be used in every situation for each situation is unique in and of itself, but a basic teaching ministry plan, by way of suggestion, would be to start with an introductory presentation of the Bible. Emphasis should be placed on what the Bible is, how it came to be, how it is organized, and how to read the Bible. From there, consideration could be given to biblical interpretations, biblical methods of explanation, the use of the Bible in daily living, how to harmonize Scriptures, and how to read the Bible with understanding.

Special emphasis could be placed on particular books of the Bible or no particular themes, doctrines, or personalities. The plan could be designed to meet specific needs at that particular time in the congregation or to address pertinent community or world issues. The objective is to have a plan and procedure and work toward implementing it in the life of the congregation.

Finally, in getting set, the pastor-teacher needs to move toward the goal. Jesus had a definite goal and purpose in mind when he saw the multitudes. He used the opportunity to seize the disciples in hearing the profound words of the kingdom. Your goal is to impart biblical truths. The means and methods will be diverse, but the goal will be constant. The methods and approaches will have to be tailor-made to fit the unique needs of your particular congregation.

To move toward the goal you will need dedicated determination and consecrated commitment. There will be times when you will feel discouraged and even feel that your feeble efforts are in vain, but you have the assurance that God's Word will not return to him void. It will accomplish the purpose according to his will.

Opening Our Mouths

Our third task as pastors-teachers is to open our mouths. To open our mouths effectively we must know what we are going to say and how to say it. The congregation assembles Sunday after Sunday with the question of King Zedekiah upon their lips, "Is there any word from the Lord?" (Jer. 37:17). Too often we as pastors give the congregation a false response that if there is, it surely is not that important or significant; if it were we would have done a better job of proclaiming it. The same holds true in the teaching ministry. The members of the flock come together for Bible study seeking biblical understanding. They are just like the Ethiopian eunuch who said to Philip, "How can I, [understand what I am reading] unless someone guides me?" (Acts 8:31). Your task as pastor-teacher is to open your mouth. Open your mouth with words of wisdom and understanding. Open your mouth with profound truths and a word of personal testimony. The congregation waits to hear what you have to say.

To open our mouths we need to speak clearly and boldly. When Jesus started his prophetic discourse upon the mountain, he did not begin by saying, "I believe I have something very important for you to hear," or "May I speak to you about the ways of the kingdom," "I sure hope what I am about to say is not offensive to you." I wonder what the disciples and the others who heard him would have thought if he had used that kind of approach? Jesus started his teaching ministry clearly and to the point. He spoke with such boldness and assurance that even his critics were mystified by his authority and ability to present eternal truths.

The pastor-teacher cannot afford to do any less in his teaching ministry. You must first be equipped and then be willing to equip the saints. You have to get your lesson together and then present it in such a manner that the congregation will be able to hear and understand. You must have congregational sensitivity in this area, for your task is to reach the people you serve, not attempt to have them reach you. Too many pastors have turned off and offended the sincere seeking of the parishioners by their approach of supreme know-it-all, rather than being chief servant, coming to share both what he knows and what he is striving to know.

Your boldness in teaching should manifest itself in your teaching method of presenting the biblical word without reservation or hesitation. To do this you must first know the biblical word. Second, believe the biblical word and third, make daily practical application of the biblical word. The expression is true, "I cannot hear what you are saying for listening to what you are doing." You cannot teach one thing and practice another. You cannot give direction to the flock and then not follow those directions yourself. Bold biblical teaching comes when you are thoroughly furnished, and you are rightly dividing the Word of truth. The Word of God is the power of the taught word, not the teacher. You as pastor-teacher are a channel through which the Word of God can once again become incarnated, and thus infiltrate the areas of ignorance, misunderstanding, and biblical illiteracy.

To open our mouths correctly we need to utilize every opportunity we have to teach God's Word. Jesus was the Master Teacher, and he used diverse and different approaches. Jesus did not use one particular teaching method as the standard. He was versatile and adaptable, using what was needed for a particular situation. Jesus would lecture, discuss, ask questions, settle arguments, point out natural observations, speak in parables, use puns, metaphors, overstatement, wisdom sayings, rebuke, or whatever was necessary to teach the people the way of the kingdom. As the pastor-teacher, you will have to develop diverse skills and adaptable methods that can be used throughout the congregation. Within most black congregations there is a unique ingathering of backgrounds and exposures. There are those with Ph.D.'s and those with no D's. The dirtiest and the elect sit side by side. The black pastor-teacher has to be a master, for he has to say something that will arouse and awaken those in the academic area, and he has to say it in such a way that "Aunt Jane" can affirm what he is saying. The success of your teaching ministry will depend on your flexibility in teaching approaches and methodologies.

Teaching Them

The fourth task of the pastor-teacher is to teach them. It was after Jesus saw the multitudes—after he was set, after he opened his mouth—that he taught them. As pastor-teacher you will have to teach (feed) the flock. Their biblical understanding and their obedience to God's will and way is directly related to your biblical understanding and how you instruct them.

To feed the flock you will have to find where they are in terms of their biblical understanding. You must be cautious in making false assumptions about their biblical maturity. Many members of the flock will be able to recite the twenty-third Psalm but not know the Shepherd of the Psalm. They will be able to verbally list the Ten Commandments but may have serious problems in understanding the Commander-in-chief. Your task will be to teach them. We do this first of all through precept and example. Your members' eagerness and enthusiasm about studying God's Word will be reflective of your study habits. If you feed the flock with prayerful and preparatory sermons with sound biblical content, your parishioners will learn to develop a high appreciation for biblical understanding. If you teach thought-provoking lessons, using biblical examples and information, the parishioners will seek and strive to obtain the information as you are giving it.

To teach them you must tell them. Simply because you are in a teaching situation where the appearance of a teaching process is in session does not mean that teaching or learning is taking place. To teach, you must have some information to impart. You need content and substance, and it must be presented in such a way that the potential learners will want to hear it and internalize it as their own. The pastor-teacher has the responsibility of bringing biblical information to the flock. If you are teaching (feeding), you will begin to see spiritual growth and maturity. Sometimes it is a seed growing secretly, but nevertheless it is growing.

To teach you have to share experience. There can be no better way to make abstract truth concrete truth than to share out of one's personal experiences. This serves to personalize and humanize the truth that one is attempting to impart. If you consider Jesus' teaching, he did this to make known eternal truths. Jesus talked about a sower and some seed. There was a woman who lost her coin, a son who left home, a landlord who went away and left his servants in charge. All of these and many more were used by the Master to personalize and internalize what he was saying.

TEACHING FROM A BIBLICAL PERSPECTIVE

"And it came to pass, when Jesus had ended these sayings, the people were astonished at his doctrine: For he taught them as one having authority, and not as the scribes" (Matt. 7:28-29, KJV).

What a summary of a teaching experience! The people were astonished. They were amazed, spellbound with surprise, for Jesus had taught them as none other.

There are specific reasons why we as pastors-teachers can teach with astonishment. I want to share them now.

   I. Basic Qualifications for a Christian Teacher
      A. Know the Scriptures (2 Tim. 2:15).
         As a Christian teacher your resource material is the Bible. You have to know it if you are going to teach from it.
      B. Embody the truth (John 14:6).
         You cannot approach biblical truths from a distance. The Word of God must be meaningful to you and become a part of you.
      C. Master the art of teaching (Mark 4:1-2).
         Skill and technique are essential. Teaching approaches and

teaching adaptability are important.
D. Believe in teaching (Matt. 4:23; 28:19-20; John 13:13).
Your ability will develop if you believe completely in what you are doing.
E. Understand human nature (John 2:24-25).
Human sensitivity is a must in the teaching ministry.
F. Desire to serve (Matt. 20:28).
The harvest is plenteous, but the laborers are few. There is much work to be done in the area of Christian education.

II. Teach for Specific Aims and Objectives
A. Convert to God (Matt. 6:33; Mark 12:30).
Your primary objective is to lead the student to a greater knowledge of who God is and what he requires.
B. Form right ideals (John 10:10; Matt. 5:1-12).
C. Fix strong convictions (John 21:15-17).
If you do not stand for something, you will fall for anything. Biblical truth needs no apology.
D. Meet life problems (2 Tim. 3:16-17).
Effective teaching is pertinent and relevant to the now situation.
E. Train for service (Matt. 4:19; 28:19-20; Mark 3:14).
You are to teach disciples, so they can teach disciples.
F. Grow mature character (Eph. 4:13).
G. Relate to others (Mark 12:31; John 13:34).
The Word of God is not taught or applied in a vacuum, but rather that others may be strengthened through its content.

III. Make Use of Teachable Materials
A. The Scriptures (2 Tim. 3:16).
There is no substitute for biblical teaching or preaching. Only the Bible is sufficient. Other materials may aid in interpretation, but there is no substitute for understanding the Word other than the Word.
B. The Natural World (Matt. 7:24-27).
Jesus used what was available and understandable to his audience. He taught by using wheat and chaff, seeds and

sheep, pearls and plants. We must do the same.

C. Current Affairs (Luke 13:1-5).

Most people know more about the present than they do about the past or the future. Make biblical application to what is going on in the contemporary world.

D. Stories (Mark 4:1-9).

There is no better way to remember truth than through the use of a story. Learn to become a good storyteller.

E. Pithy Sayings (Matt. 6:21; 12:30; Mark 4:24).

Much truth can be contained in a small declaration. You do not have to teach a lesson for a long period of time. Just teach it to the point.

F. Figures of Speech (Prov. 25:11; Matt. 23:37; John 15:1-10).

Using the language of the people helps in communicating something which otherwise may sound or seem completely foreign to them.

G. Concrete Statements (Matt. 5:13-14).

The truth plainly and precisely spoken carries much weight. Tell it just as it is.

IV. Procedures in a Lesson

A. Introduction

You need to have a starting point that will arouse interest and enthusiasm in what you are about to teach. The introduction should be your point of contact, accepting the students where they are as they are, moving them to where you are trying to get them to go. You should explain to the student what you are going to teach and why it is important to learn what is before them.

B. Securing the Point of Contact

You should start the lesson where the student is and move them in a progressive manner toward ascertaining the content information. The point of contact is where the wave length of what you have to teach and what the student wants to learn meets.

C. Development

Your concerns in this area are presentation, procedures,

motivating interest, teaching in an understandable manner, being precise enough to stay with the lesson aim and plan, and yet flexible enough to include outside interests or thoughts.

The best way to develop the lesson is to first have clear what you are going to teach, how you will teach it, what measuring or evaluative instrument you will use to determine whether you have accomplished your aim or not. There can be no substitute for lesson preparation. Too often in Christian education the "just any" attitude prevails. What are you going to teach? Just anything. When are you going to teach? Just anytime. Where are you going to teach? Just anywhere. Our Lord and Master certainly did not take this teaching approach. In the fullness of time he came; when he was set he opened his mouth; after the disciples and multitudes assembled, he taught them. We as pastors-teachers cannot afford to do any less.

D. Application

The lesson must be made relevant and pertinent to the students' needs if it is to have meaning. To simply talk remotely about what a biblical character did or did not know or teach about what the Lord commands without making personal and practical application is futile.

When Jesus was asked the question, Who is my neighbor? he gave the answer in a story form about an injured man by the wayside. For Jesus to have told about a Levite, a priest, a Samaritan, and an injured traveler without applying the truths to his audience would have made the whole story of little consequence.

Application takes place when the lesson is internalized in the student, becoming a part of one's thinking and behavior.

E. Evaluation

You should have some instrument to measure and determine if what was taught was learned. Just because you taught the lesson does not mean that learning has taken place. One of the surest ways of evaluating a lesson, especially a Bible lesson that is taught in an informal nonstructured situation, is to ask questions. You may want to use written questions or thoughts to be shared for discussion purposes. Of course the ultimate evaluative instrument is the life that is lived and the fruit that comes forth from the teaching-learning exercise. More will be said about this process of the lesson at the end of the chapter.

Teaching Methodologies

The pastor-teacher should have basic understanding of teaching dynamics and methodologies if he is to correctly and effectively teach the teachers and teach the flock.

There are about five basic steps that should be considered as the pastor-teacher leads the flock in the ministry of teaching.

Aims and Objectives

Findley B. Edge, in *Teaching for Results,* states that the aim of the lesson is the goal you are trying to reach, the target you are shooting for, the results you are seeking to bring forth. There are three kinds of aims. They are the knowledge, inspiration, and conduct response aims. It is a knowledge aim if the dominant purpose of the teacher is to lead the class in a logical, systematic, intensive study of a body of knowledge and to lead to a mastery of that knowledge. "An example would be 'To lead my class members to master the essential facts in the Genesis account of creation.'"[11] It is an inspiration aim if the dominant purpose of the teacher is to lead the class to have a deeper appreciation of some Christian truth or to lead the class to accept or reaccept some generalized ideal. Example, "To lead my class members to have a deeper social consciousness." It is a conduct response aim if the dominant purpose of the teacher is to lead individuals to begin to express in a specific way some Christian action in daily life. This action or response must be observable, and it is preferable if the individual can begin practicing it immediately. It is an observable Christian response in life. An example is "To lead my class to sponsor a recreation program for our young people."[12]

There are three things an aim ought to do:

1. *Be brief enough to remember. As a teacher you need to know what you are attempting to teach and be able to say it just as precise and to the point as you can.*

2. *Specific enough to be applied. You cannot teach in the abstract. You have to teach in the concrete. State specifically what it is you are saying and make it realistic enough to be done or believed.*
3. *Detailed enough to be understood. You should tell yourself and your students what it is you are striving to achieve. Whether you get there or not will depend upon many factors, but you should at least know where you are going.*

The pastor-teacher should keep in mind that the aim is what he is trying to bring out through the working of the Holy Spirit.

Developing the Lesson

After the lesson aim has been determined and defined, the pastor-teacher should move in the area of developing the lesson to accomplish the lesson aim. To do this, you need to develop a lesson plan.

The lesson plan consists of the lesson aim, purposeful and meaningful Bible study, class discussion and participation, personal application and evaluation.

The pastor-teacher should start the lesson where the class is located as pertaining to the biblical understanding.

Feeding the Feeders (Teachers)

The pastor-teacher may ask the question, "How do we share with the teachers the methodology we have acquired?"

This can be done through the weekly officers and teachers meeting. The pastor-teacher should keep in mind that there are four areas in which the teachers need help.

1. The teachers need help in the area of Bible knowledge. The teachers cannot teach the Bible until they first have a working understanding of the Bible and the contents therein. The teachers instrument is the Bible. That instrument must be used with skill and proper application.

2. The teachers need help in theology. Theology is basically our thinking or thoughts about God. This thinking about God has to be biblically correct because from our theology we develop our biblical doctrines. Most teachers and some pastors are weak when it comes to

understanding biblical doctrines, that is, what the Bible teaches or says about certain beliefs and practices. There is a real challenge that the pastor-teacher will encounter in this area, for most people will know more about their culture than their Christ, more about their tradition than about the truth. Bible study will help to alleviate this problem.

3. The teachers need help in understanding age group characteristics. The teachers need to have sensitivity to the age group with whom they are to work. You cannot approach every lesson the same way at the same understanding level. Jesus showed how diverse and adaptable we should become as teachers to teach the eternal truth. The point should be emphasized that we have to adapt to our students. They, for the most part, cannot, and will not adapt to us.

4. The teachers need help in improving their teaching methodologies. For the most part, those who give themselves to the teaching ministry in the local church, are good lay people who probably work in a job that is drastically different from teaching the other six days of the week. They must be trained as Christian teachers.

The Weekly Officers and Teachers Meeting

The primary objective of this meeting is the improvement of the teachers.

The Organizational Structure—Suggested

1. Fellowship Hour—6:00-6:30

    This can be a meal prepared by someone who is not a teacher and served to make it as convenient as possible for the teachers to attend. The fellowship meal serves to enhance oneness and a bond of Christian love, as teachers come together to do a specific task.

2. Promotional Period—6:30-6:45

    This time would be used by the church school director, minister of education, superintendent, or pastor. The secretary's report would be read, stating teachers' presence or absence, what has been done, and what needs to be done. The goal of the lesson unit would be stressed and direction would be given.

3. Departmental Period—6:45-7:00

    The departmental superintendents would meet with

their department teachers giving specific directions and concerns. Class enrollment, teacher morale, the quarter's objectives, the work of the Sunday School should all be discussed at this time. Departmental promotions and special concerns of the department would be considered.

4. Teacher Improvement Period—7:00-8:00

During this period, teaching methodologies, film-strips, the use of audiovisuals in the teaching process, how to arrange the class, correlating previous lessons, etc. The biblical lesson is presented, preparing the teachers to teach next Sunday's lesson.

The study of the lesson should be done with consideration to age divisions. If the teaching staff is adequate enough to do so, the lesson could be taught at different locations according to interest and need.

The weekly teachers' meeting should be a continual school for teacher training. Give the teachers the information and then give them an opportunity to practice what you have given them.

TECHNIQUES FOR EVALUATING BIBLE STUDY

My mother always said, "The proof of the pudding is in the tasting." The concern of the pastor-teacher is how to "taste" effectively.

You as pastor-teacher may have all of the ingredients: teachers, staff persons, physical plant, materials, and a willing heart, but how do you know whether you are accomplishing anything? You must evaluate. You want to see what it is you are doing and what needs to be done. Simply because a lesson has been taught does not mean that a lesson has been learned.

There are instruments you can use to "taste" your Bible study effectiveness.

Measuring Cognitive Outcome

The cognitive is that which is knowable and observable.

A. Paper and Pencil Tests

1. *True/False Questions and Statements.* Most Bible classes are infor-

mal and nonstructured. In this light, the true/false test can be effective in getting direct answers to measure whether the students learned what was before them.

Example: there are sixty-six books in the Bible. ____ True ____ False

2. *Fill in the Blank.* Short statements with most of the information given, and the student supplying the missing part.

Example: Jesus had ____ disciples.

3. *Multiple Choice.* A statement is given with the facts before the students. They are asked to determine the correct answer.

Example: Which book is not a Gospel? A. Matthew C. Peter
                                          B. John   D. Luke

4. *Constructed Response*

a. Short Answers. These would be short questions or statements that the students would elaborate on.

Example: Where was Jesus born?

b. *Fill-in.* Give a statement or question with most of the information. Have the student supply the missing part.

Example: Matthew was a tax collector.

Peter was a _____ .

5. *Alternative-Response.* The question or statement would be presented with the choice of deciding yes or no, right or wrong, agree or disagree, is or is not, true or false.

Example: Jesus turned water into wine in Capernaum.

6. *Matching.* The student is asked to match or correlate the correct words or statements.

Example: ____ 1. Joshua   1. Deacon
            ____ 2. Judas   2. Luke
            ____ 3. Philip   3. Battle of Jericho
            ____ 4. Gospel   4. Betrayer

7. *Rearrangement.* The objective is to have the students put in chronological order or sequence the given information.

Example: List the major prophets as they appear in the Bible. Put in sequence in the life of Jesus—baptizing, temptation, calling of disciples, prayer in Gethsemane.

8. *Creative Games.* Role playing and the acting out of biblical lessons can be a useful instrument to observe and measure the level of comprehension of the class members.

The pastor-teacher should be flexible enough to utilize a number of evaluative measurements to determine his effectiveness as a teacher. He also should teach the teachers these techniques that the sheep might be thoroughly fed.

There was a time when the black pastor was the most educated man in the congregation and often in the community. The sun has set on that day and seemingly will never rise again.

The pastor-teacher for these times must be a specialist. He need not feel inferior, nor apologize for his specialized training. He must be astute in the biblical word and sound in the Christian doctrine. There will be many professional members of the flock, but when it is time to feed the flock, the pastor-teacher will have to come forward as God's man with God's Word for God's people.

4
The Pastor as Healer

The Spirit of the Lord is upon me, because he hath . . . sent me to heal the brokenhearted (Luke 4:18, KJV).

THE BIBLICAL BASE FOR MINISTRY TO THE SICK

The Nature of Ministry to the Sick in the Old Testament.
  Agents of Healing
  Priest-Physician Relations—The early priests are generally accepted as the first physicians, although some scholars have questioned this position, since society was a patriarchal character.[1] The secret practices of magical medicine were conserved by the priests, and priestly medicine developed by logical necessity. These early priest-physicians have also been called witch doctors and medicine men, performing the functions of the pastor, doctor, and scientist in a rudimentary fashion. The duties and powers of the medicine man always varied according to the intellectual plane of the tribe. As the organization and life of the tribe became more complex, there was a simple kind of specialization. In order to reach his objective he had to distract the patient's attention from the suffering, inspire confidence, and leave a token of his healing power.[2]
  Sources of Knowledge of Hebrew Medicine—The main sources of knowledge concerning ancient Hebrew medicine are the Bible and the Talmud. These sources mentioned medicine only in the course of historical narratives, or when it elucidated some legal or ceremonial matter. There were no special medical treatises, but certain medical regulations, statements, and suggestions scattered throughout the

109

various books. No Hebrew medical books are extant dating prior to the seventh century BC. The Talmud transmitted an abundance of medical conceptions of medicine.[3] The Talmud makes mention of "the medical book" which it ascribes to King Solomon and mentions that it was hidden by Hezekiah.[4] Later, Gentile writers referred to early Hebrew efforts in the field of medicine. Aulus Celsus, writing in the first century AD, referred to two medicines which were introduced by earlier Hebrew Physicians.

The Priest as Public Health Officer—Prior to the time of Moses, there were indications that the head of the family or patriarch was both priest and physician as well as judge. Abraham, Isaac, and Jacob held the power of blessing and birthright in addition to performing the rite of circumcision. The story of Job had a similar patriarchal setting and pictured Job as sanctifying his children and offering sacrifice on their behalf. Gradually these priestly and medical powers fell into the hands of individuals who formed communities or societies.[5]

The majority of the material relating to the medical functions of the priests was naturally conserved by the priestly tradition. One of the primary functions of the priest was to interpret the Torah, which was as timeless as the word of the prophet. It was natural that the personality of Moses, the unique lawgiver, would act as a magnet in gathering the law into a homogenous whole. It is natural to assume that Moses' first thoughts on preventive medicine and state sanitation came from his contacts in Egypt. According to the Book of Acts, Moses was "instructed in all the wisdom of the Egyptians."[6] It is exceedingly probable that he saw many of the evil diseases of Egypt so frequently mentioned in the Pentateuch. During his pastoral life in Midian, he must have gathered much about tribal life, customs, and habits of the desert. There he also observed nature, making deductions concerning what was fit and unfit for human consumption. By watching his flock, he probably learned much about eugenics, recognizing the bad effects of inbreeding.[7]

It seems highly probable that the homework for the system of sanitation found in the Pentateuch was incorporated by Moses into the daily life of the children of Israel.

According to the holiness code of Leviticus, there was a special relationship between cleanliness and godliness. Because physical purity was placed on a par with moral purity, the hygienic regulations had the characteristics of religious precepts and ritual ceremonies. The duty of strict cleanliness was laid upon the people, not entirely because of the specific danger of disease but because to be clean was acceptable in the eyes of God.[8] The priests were thus specifically charged with the administration of hygienic requirements and the guardianship of the moral, spiritual, and physical well-being of the people.

The Priest as Diagnostician—The second phase of the medical duties assigned to the priests covered contagious diseases. Their job was again administrative, as supervisors in all cases of suspected contagious disease. The priest in Israel had no authority to treat diseases in general. Their main jurisdiction seems to have been over those suffering from edemic diseases.[9] The priestly tradition gave elaborate directions in the thirteenth, fourteenth, and fifteenth chapters of Leviticus, so the priest might recognize certain diseases and then be able to determine later whether they had been cured. There is no reference to a priest giving any treatment, medical, magical, or by exorcism. His duty was to decide whether the patient was to be banished from the social life of the community, or whether he might be readmitted. Since the exclusion or admission carried with it the right to religious worship in the tabernacle, Temple, or synagogue, it was inevitable that the priest would have the final decision. During the ministry of Jesus, the priest was still the final judge as to whether the leper was cured and whether he could be admitted to the synagogue.[10]

According to very ancient Jewish tradition, the priests called on physicians when they were personally sick. The Talmud referred to Temple physicians appointed to treat the priests, who were often troubled with abdominal pains and arthritis from the daily oblations in cold water and standing barefoot on cold stones.[11]

The priest therefore had a twofold medical duty, as public health officer and diagnostician. Unlike other ancient peoples, the priests did not monopolize the art of healing but were restricted to a narrow field. Sacrifices and offerings were the only means of treatment authorized for their use. However, the priests were of great importance in the administration of sanitation and control of contagious disease.

GOD AS SUPREME HEALER

Divine Origin of Health

The concept that healing is of divine origin was deeply noted in all Hebrew thought, even becoming a part of the daily ritual. The effect of the monotheistic concept in Israel was of prime importance as the function of healing was ascribed solely to God. The one God was the source of all disease and all health, either directly or indirectly. Basic to the idea of God as healer was the concept of God's conservation of nature. The Hebrew not only recognized that he created the world but that his creative activity was continuous. God was directly behind every event in nature and there was no place in the Hebrew mind for a series of secondary causes.[12] Since God was actively concerned with all his creation, it was natural for the Hebrews to recognize him as the supreme sustainer of health. This concept was not separate from their view of life and creation, but it was basic to their understanding of God's continuing activity.

According to the tradition, the place of God in the healing process was impressed upon the children of Israel at Marah, their first stopping place after leaving the Red Sea. Here they were taught their first lesson about their peculiar character as a nation.

> There the Lord made for them a statute and an ordinance and there he proved them, saying, "If you will diligently hearken to the voice of the Lord your God, and do that which is right in his eyes, and give heed to his commandments and keep all his statutes, I will put none of the diseases upon you which I put upon the Egyptians; for I am the Lord your healer."[13]

The basic nature and primary place of this passage is apparent because it seems to be the first statute or ordinance given after the marvelous events of their escape from bondage in Egypt. A similar idea was repeated at Sinai as the promise was found in a more general form:

> You shall serve the Lord your God, and I will bless your bread and your water; and I will take sickness away from the midst of you.[14]

In the song of Moses there was a similar refrain, emphasizing the place of God as healer. Here Moses was speaking for God:

> See now that I, even I, am he, and there is no god besides me;/I kill
> and I make alive; I wound and I heal;/and there is none that can
> deliver out of my hand.[15]

The passages from the Pentateuch lay a framework within the law which determined the orthodox position on healing and health for the people of Israel. However, the emphasis upon God as supreme healer did not end here. Many references demonstrate this standard of orthodoxy.

Eliphaz reminded Job, "He wounds, but he binds up; he smites, but his hands heal."[16] The psalmist stated that "The Lord sustains him on his sickbed; in his illness thou healest all his infirmities."[17] Another passage in the Psalter bore this same theme: "Bless the Lord, O my soul, and forget not all his benefits,/who forgives all your iniquity, who heals all your diseases."[18] Hosea voiced his assurance as he said, "Come, let us return to the Lord;/for he has torn, that he may heal us;/ he has stricken and he will bind us up."[19]

The ability of God to heal was likewise revealed in the many promises of healing. It is important to see the various uses of the verb, *ropho*, to heal. The root idea appeared to refer to "serving together" or "mending," first a wound and then a disease. The resultant meaning was hence "to heal."[20] The word was used in a literal sense to convey the medical idea, "to make whole or well." The writer of Proverbs emphasized this by coupling healing with flesh and medicine with bones:

> Trust in the Lord with all your heart, and do not rely upon your own
> insight./In all your ways acknowledge him, and he will make straight
> your paths./Be not wise in your own eyes; fear the Lord, and turn
> away from evil./It will be healing to your flesh and refreshment to
> your bones.[21]

The verb was also used metaphorically in relation to the restoration of soul. Jeremiah illustrated this as he repeated:

> For I will restore health to you, and your wounds will I heal, says the
> Lord,/because they have called you an outcast: "It is Zion, for whom
> no one cares!"[22]

A passage in the writings of the Chronicles illustrated still another use of the verb as it applied to the healing of the land.

*If my people who are called by name humble themselves, and pray
and seek my face, and turn from their wicked ways, then I will hear
from heaven, and will forgive their sin and heal their land.*[23]

In general, the Old Testament taught that good health resulted
from holy living and was a divine gift of God. Healing of disease was
likewise God's gift and was based on forgiveness, intercession, and
sometimes sacrifice. The seeking of health from Yahweh was considered the definite duty of an individual.[24]

The point of greatest significance in the Hebrew concept of
healing lies in the overall view of God's place in the healing process.
There were those in Old Testament days who magnified this to the
complete exclusion of human instrumentality. At the same time, a
more balanced view of God's place was developing and found expression in the writings of Jesus ben Sirach. He declared that the physician
was an instrument of God who was or should be working in accord with
and not against the purposes of God. The true physician was viewed as
endowed with power of God, and his remedies owed their potency to
God. The physician was to pray for God's blessing upon his patient and
upon his treatment. The patient was to fulfill his duty to God by
forsaking his sin and praying for God's healing to be accomplished
through the physician.[25]

What a sharp contrast this presents to the materialistic tendency
in modern medicine. Today, one first calls the physician, gets a
prescription, and then calls the minister to pray for the sick. In a very
real sense, neither the physician nor his medicine ever heals. The
prescribed treatment only stimulates the natural functions or removes
what hinders them. Even when treated by dressings of a physician,
every cut heals itself, and the same treatment does not heal in a similar
wound in a deceased person. The biochemical energy which heals in a
live body proceeds from God as Creator and Sustainer of life. C. S.
Lewis has expressed it in this way:

> All who are cured are cured by Him, not merely in the sense
> that His providence provides them with medical assistance and
> wholesome environment, but also in the sense that their very
> tissues are repaired by the far-descended energy, which flowing
> from His energies, the whole system of nature.[26]

MINISTRY TO THE SICK IN THE NEW TESTAMENT

In the days of his earthly ministry, Jesus' hands were ever outstretched to heal.

Jesus came with an active compassion of intense spiritual energy and set about to give men life, and that in abundance. Healing power flowed out from him like a stream of fresh water on the arid souls and tortured bodies of suffering humanity.[27] Matthew notes that in the very dawn of his ministry "Jesus went about all Galilee, teaching in their synagogues, and preaching the gospel of the kingdom, and healing all manner of sickness and all manner of disease among the people."[28]

Later, after many healing miracles had been performed by Jesus, Matthew states that these were healed "That it might be fulfilled which was spoken by Esaias the prophet, saying, Himself took our infirmities, and bare our sicknesses.[29] Following this, Matthew gives many instances of healing of every kind and declares once again that "Jesus went about all the cities and villages, teaching in their synagogues, and preaching the gospel of the kingdom, and healing every sickness and every disease among the people."[30] Thus it is clearly evident from the historical record of the work of Jesus in the realm of human experience that it was his obvious intention to use his divine energy in the restoring, upbuilding and completing of lives of people.

Nevertheless, Jesus would not be known as a mere wonder-worker, or as a mendicant leader.

His great task was the bringing of the crippled in body and soul into an ever growing fellowship with the Father, whether it was by curing their broken bodies or by preaching the gospel of repentance.[31]

It is immediately perceived that healing formed a vital part of the work of redemption. It was exemplified in Jesus' ministry. It was included in his commissions, and it was practiced by his followers.

Exemplified in the Healing Ministry of Jesus

Even to the casual student of the Gospels it is evident that Jesus gave a great portion of his time to the ministry of healing. A close examination reveals that at least twenty-five of the thirty-five miracles are healing miracles.[32] In the beginning of his great Galilean ministry

Jesus healed a demoniac in the synagogue in Capernaum.[33] From there he made his way to Peter's home where he cured Peter's mother-in-law of fever.[34] On the evening of the same day Jesus healed many that were brought to Peter's door.[35] From this time, physical healing had an important place in the activity of Jesus.

He healed the leper,[36] the centurion's servant,[37] the paralytic,[38] the man with the withered hand,[39] a woman who had suffered from an issue of blood for twelve years,[40] and on another occasion a woman who had been afflicted with a "spirit of infirmity" for eighteen years.[41]

On the Sabbath day he healed the lame man at the pool of Bethesda,[42] a man with the dropsy,[43] the man born blind,[44] and others.[45] Jesus cleansed the lepers,[46] and exorcised demons. Finally, in the garden, he restored the ear of Malchus.[47]

In addition to these specific cases of healing, there are at least eighteen passages that either give a summary account of the healing of Jesus or make some reference to it. Often the record speaks of the pursuing multitudes pressing about him, all anxiously awaiting His word that would restore their withered limbs and give sight to their blinded eyes.[48] Thus it is not inappropriate to speak of him as "the Great Physician"; neither is it difficult to see that healing held an eminent place in the ministry of Jesus. Harnack says, "Our Lord's ministry of healing appears as His characteristic work.[49]

Why Did Jesus Heal?

In no other realm in the ministry of the Master is his sovereignty as apparent as in his healing ministry. He was sovereign in the places he chose to visit and perform his power of healing. He asserted his sovereignty in regard to the persons whom he chose to heal. *He did not go everywhere, and he did not heal everybody.*

Counting Christ's healings in the largest possible numbers, one still must recognize that such a group was infinitesimally small in comparison with the millions in Palestine and over the earth.

In other words, if compassion for the multitudes in connection with their physical condition was the chief constraint upon Jesus in his healing acts, his life and ministry must remain an enigma.[50]

It would seem that compassion was not the chief constraint in his healing, *but it was his desire to reveal his divine person and power and his ultimate purpose and mission.*

Though Jesus reacted strongly against the prevailing messianic ideas of glory and dominion by way of the miraculous,[51] he nevertheless used some of his healing miracles as indications of his messiahship.

Though Jesus identified himself as Messiah through his works of healing, his failure to use his power for Jewish nationalists' ends disappointed the multitudes and angered the Jewish leaders.

A second reason Jesus performed miracles of healing was *to validate his personal claims.* That Jesus had established himself with his apostles in being all that he claimed to be is seen clearly in statements made by Peter and others after his ascension. While here on earth Jesus had claimed to be able to forgive sin, and he proved his right to do so by saying to the sick of the palsy, "Take up thy bed, and go."[52] He proved he was the Light of the world by bringing sight to the blind.[53] In the healing of the woman with an issue of blood Jesus emphasized that he had within himself power which healed and restored.[54]

Finally, it would seem that Jesus *performed miracles of healings and parabolic illustrations of his ultimate purpose of complete redemption of all who came to him by faith.* His healings were of evidential value not only to those upon whom they were performed and those who witnessed them but to men of every age. Thus, in the exorcism of the demons and the healing of their victims, Jesus showed his power to set men free from the power of spiritual evil. With the healing of the blind he was teaching that sight would be given to all who seek in faith and are willing to receive it. His redemptive work was to give men life and free them from the shackles of sin. His longing to consummate his redemptive work and his final purpose of undoing once and forever the ravages of sin, not only as against the soul but also the body, is clearly manifested in his miracles of healing.

These would seem to be some of the deeper motives for the healing ministry of Jesus. Perhaps there are many more but on no occasion did he use physical suffering or his own power to overcome it as a means to an end, to gain an audience, to create a friendly atmosphere, or to give dramatic proof of his messiahship. Rather, his response was instinctive, a spontaneous outgoing of sympathy and love.

In his incarnation, the Lord, one with the love and compassion of the Father, identified himself with the sufferings and sorrow of men.

The Permanency of the Healing Ministry

Healing formed an essential part of the work and teaching of Jesus Christ and of his ministry of the early church.

The Jews had expected one who would heal their diseases and bear their infirmities.[55] Jesus appeared among his people as a "physician."[56] Mark and Luke both record his words given in response to the Pharisees who had criticized his association with publicans and sinners. He declared, "They that are whole have no need of the physician, but they that are sick."[57] The first three Gospels depict him as the physician of the body and soul, as Savior and healer of men. Jesus says very little about sickness; he cures it.

Repeatedly Jesus was surrounded by crowds of sick people.[58] They approached him as individuals who were ceremonially unclean, covered with the loathsome disease of leprosy.[59] No sickness of the soul or body repelled him. He touched the blinded eyes, the deaf ears, and the leprous skin. He rebuked the fever, the epilepsy, and the demons. He caused withered hands, strengthless feet, and twisted bodies to be restored. Personalities were maladjusted, and the value of the individual was greatly discounted. Jesus walked among them keeping always vital and pure. He healed all who came.

Jesus sent out the twelve and the seventy charging them to "go, preach, saying, The Kingdom of heaven is at hand. Heal the sick, cleanse the lepers, raise the dead, cast out devils: freely ye have received, freely give."[60]

Peter and the other apostles began at Pentecost to do "many wonders and signs."[61] Peter healed the lame man at the Beautiful Gate,[62] and he healed Aeneas at Lydda.[63]

That Paul considered healing an integral part of the church's program is clearly evident from his words in 1 Corinthians. He stated that God had given to some "the gifts of healing."[64] James[65] asserted that the health of the body should be a chief concern of the church by indicating the procedure that should be followed when one was sick. Paul and James brought the matter up in a very casual way indicating that it was a very natural part of the work, and there was not a question as to its permanence or place in the program of Christianity.

It may be logically concluded: healing was not a transitory characteristic of Christianity which served only in the establishment of the Christian religion; rather, it was given as a permanent and abiding commission to the church of every age.

The church must go back to the beginning and take up her commission afresh and do as the Lord commanded: preach the gospel and heal the sick. Such a conclusion is staggering in importance. The church cannot ignore these facts. Pastoral work with the sick has always been a ministry of the church.

The Holistic Ministry

The black pastor's ministry of healing to his parishioners must be total in its scope. Because black people look to their pastor as an "absolute" person, his ministry to them must be absolute. There can be no categorizing or selective avenues of ministry that the black pastor can take, for surely he must be all things to all of his people.

The community at large has a network of possibilities that a person can choose for specific assistance in almost all areas of life. For the black community these channels, when present, are very randomly and haphazardly used. When black people need counseling, their first inclination is not to seek a professional counselor or a counseling agency but rather their pastor, peer group person, or family member. When black people need to know what agencies are available to help them with a specific problem, they will usually check with their pastor or at least someone in their church who may be of assistance.

The black pastor's task is to work with the body, mind, soul, will, emotions, and interests of his people. He cannot afford to dichotomize his people or their needs.

Jesus is our best example in developing and having a holistic ministry. When Jesus saw eyes that were blind or a mind that was confused, he saw the person. When he encountered the woman at Jacob's well or was challenged to deal with the woman brought to him who was caught in adultery, he saw their sinfulness and brokenness, within the personhood context.

Our danger is that we seek to categorize or divide persons according to their descriptions and desires, but Jesus saw persons worth saving, persons worth loving, even persons worth dying for. He did not selectively list their needs and say this is a social need, that is a spiritual need.

As we seek to minister in the holistic context, we must be ever mindful of this fact. As black pastors, our people come to us with their needs, their hurts, their fears, their desires, and their failures. There are no grounds of their existence that should be considered as off limits to us. I do not want to give the impression that we have God's OK to take his place and play his role, nor do I want us to believe that we are experts and masters in all areas of life—let me say profoundly, we are not. What I do mean to say is that as black pastors, our task is to be sensitive to the needs and hurts of our people and do all in our power to minister to them as God gives us direction and understanding.

The Ministry of Touch

For the black pastor to be affective and effective as a healing minister, seeking to make the entire person whole, he must touch persons where they are. God in Christ showed us that the way to minister unto persons is to come where they are and deal with them as they are.

The black pastor must have an incarnational ministry. He must be real flesh and blood among his people. We will never heal people by remote control or at a distance from them.

Once again, no area of our people's existence should be considered off limits to us.

To have the ministry of touch we must see the person who needs our help. The indictment against the Levite and priest, as Jesus taught about who was a good neighbor, was that for their convenient purposes they did not "see" the wounded man. They simply passed over him and kept going.

To bring the ministry of healing to a place of effective service we must see our people, see them not as we want them to be but see them as they really are.

After we see them we must know them. Jesus talked to the woman at the well about her greatest need. He saw her as she was, and he knew her need. At the surface level it may have appeared that all she needed was physical water and nothing else, but at the soul level she needed a spring of everlasting water. Jesus knew this, and he dealt with her at her level of greatest need.

We cannot minister to our people until we see them and know their level of greatest need. Too often we get sidetracked talking about the weather when our people want to know how they are going to make it through the storms of life.

When we have seen them and know them, we must move toward them by reaching out. Jesus reached out. He did not set up office hours telling the people when he was in, but rather his office was among the people, and his hours were "whenever you need me, call me."

To minister as a healer, being used by God's grace, we must emulate Jesus at these levels.

We must see our people, know our people, and then be willing to reach out to our people.

This ministry may take us to huts or havens, along highways or down dirt roads, but wherever the people are, there we must be.

We must bring compassion and concern and leave behind selfishness and social status. Our task is to visit, "heal the brokenhearted," bind up the wounded, and to restore the perishing?

The Black Pastor as Visitor

> Therefore thus saith the Lord God of Israel against the pastors that feed my people; Ye have scattered my flock, and driven them away, and have not visited them: behold, I will visit upon you the evil of your doings, saith the Lord (Jer. 23:2, KJV).
> I was sick, and ye visited me: I was in prison, and ye came unto me (Matt. 25:36, KJV).

Clearly the biblical bases is established for a ministry of visitation.

The word of the Lord to Jeremiah was that the Lord was about to bring judgment upon the pastors because they had neglected their responsibility of visiting God's people.

The words of Jesus in Matthew's Gospel show the supreme importance that Jesus placed upon the ministry of visitation. In fact,

one of the criteria for being chosen as the blessed of the Lord will be by
those who have visited and cared for the people.

We need to understand that the word *visit* is more than just our
casual use of the word, merely dropping by or going over to see
someone; rather, the Hebrew word for visit—*pokad*—means to show
concern for or to oversee the affairs of the other.

When we visit we bring the presence of Christ to bear upon that
particular situation. We show both his and our compassion and
concern. We represent the church and the Christian community as we
seek to be the Lord's ambassadors.

All visits are not the same and should therefore be treated as such.

I want to share with you some of the many types of visits the
pastor is called upon to make.

Church Visitation

Purpose: this would be general visitation to members of the
congregation to establish pastoral relationships, seeking to involve the
member in the total work of the church and seeking to oversee the
member in spiritual growth and development.

Methods:
A. Establish a system of visiting in the home of as many members
as possible. This is vitally important for a new pastor to get to know his
members as best he can. By going to the homes of members he can
begin to develop a pastoral-personal relationship. I say this that way
because the pastor should develop personal relationships, but he
should keep those personal relationships in perspective. He does not
and should not cease to be the pastor, to be personal with a member.

Parish visitation in the home is necessary for the pastor who has
served a congregation for some time because it keeps him abreast of his
people and sensitive to their needs.

B. Seek deeper involvement and participation in the life of the
church.

In parish visitation the pastor should visit with specific objectives
in mind. His purpose should be to involve the members in more of the
work of the church and discover what gifts or talents they have that can
enhance the kingdom program.

C. Affirm the presence of Christ in the affairs of the people.

The pastor should be sensitive and warm to his people when he visits, but he should keep the conversation and the visit in pastoral perspective. I do not mean that he should not smile or be humorous, or that he has to be so rigid that he makes everyone uncomfortable that he is there. I do believe he should let it be known through word and action that he has come ultimately on the Lord's business.

D. Establish a personal relationship.

It is all right to get personal with your members as long as you keep it in a pastoral perspective. Seek to identify with the person, rather than have the person try to identify with you. When Jesus talked with fishermen he identified with them. When he talked with a thirsty Samaritan woman, he identified with her.

E. Respond to invitations.

Members of the congregation will invite the pastor to their homes for dinner or social activities. Take advantage of these opportunities to get closer to your people. Once again, keep the visit in pastoral perspective. There are times when members will have the pastor over to get his opinion or his support on a church issue. Watch and pray at these times.

Visiting the Sick at Home

Purpose: the pastor goes to oversee the condition and circumstances that the member is in, bringing the healing power of Christ's presence to bear upon the situation. As he makes a sick visit at home, the pastor brings the resources of the church, both help and hope, that the sick might be restored to health.

Methods:

1. Inform the member(s) you are going to visit.

This can be done by having a regular day when you make home visitations or selected hours of the day that you are on the church field. Make the visitation announcement from the pulpit or put it in the church bulletin or newsletter when sick members at home can expect a pastoral visit.

I am aware that in a very large church there may be a hundred or more persons who need a pastoral visit. Physically this is impossible to do, but it is still the pastor's responsibility to make the visit. Keep in mind the biblical use of the word *visit,* to oversee, showing concern for the other. To see that this work does not go lacking, the pastor should call upon the deacons, the missionary groups of the church, the concerned members of the congregation, and if the field is large enough and the work load too demanding, additional ministerial staff persons should be used.

I cannot stress too strongly that it is the pastor's responsibility to care for the flock.

2. Make the visit when scheduled.

There is no use having a scheduled time of visitation and then not come at the expected time. If you are unable to keep a scheduled home visit, notify the person as soon as possible, and if possible reschedule another time then.

3. Be sensitive to the home situation.

You are the pastor of the flock, not the head of each individual family. There are times when it will not be conducive to a pastoral visit, that is, a family dispute, a party in progress, the family just beginning a meal, and many other situations the pastor will have to be sensitive to.

4. Make a visit.

Keep in perspective that your task is to care for and oversee the concerns of your congregation. You do not go to a sick room to give or get the gossip but to share the gospel.

5. Leave your personal feelings about your health and yourself to yourself.

The sick person is concerned about the pastor's well-being, but more importantly, the pastor comes to minister and not be ministered unto. It is one of the blessed consequences of pastoral ministry that as we give ourselves, so we also receive.

6. Be brief, but not in a hurry.

Each situation will bring about flexibility in the time of the visit. You should not automatically set a fixed time and then work to keep it. That becomes mechanical and unreal. You should be time conscious and member-condition conscious as you visit.

7. If possible, take a deacon or other member with you, especially into the home of single, divorced, or a widow who lives alone. "Abstain from all appearance of evil" (1 Thess. 5:22, KJV).

8. Have a word of prayer.

You make your visit as an ambassador for Christ. Let his presence and his power be known through the channel of prayer. You should be sensitive that in every situation, every time you visit, you do not have to pray out loud or publicly.

9. If you plan on coming again, let this be known. If not, do not mention it.

One of the quickest ways to lose pastoral credibility is to promise your member(s) something and then not come through.

Visiting the Shut-in

Purpose: The pastor goes to oversee the condition and circumstances of the shut-in member. His objective in this ministry is to see that the shut-in member does not become a shut-out member. Systematic visiting is vitally important, because the shut-in person is usually confined for a long period of time.

Methods:

1. Establish a pattern or schedule of visitation. You need not inform the member of this schedule but you need to have some organization to your visitation routine. This prevents you from going to some homes or institutions too frequently while neglecting others all together.

2. The key is to build a continual relationship.

You will be visiting this person on many occasions. The sooner you can establish a personal-pastor relationship, the better.

3. Keep them informed of church activities.

You may want to mail a weekly bulletin to them. Send them Sunday School or other Christian education literature.

4. Refer them to other avenues of ministry.

Quality television programs, religious radio broadcasts, newspapers, religious journals and pamphlets, church bulletins, and newsletters.

5. Be cautious not to pacify them but be sure to minister to them.

Read the Holy Scriptures, share a thought, have a word of prayer, give them specific persons and needs they can pray for. If they are able to use the telephone, give them the name and telephone number of other shut-in persons they can minister to while being confined themselves.

6. If you are going away on vacation or for any reason for a period of time, inform them of this. The shut-in member has been left enough. They need not feel left by the pastor.

7. Remember them on special days.

Their birthday (if you know it), Christmas, church anniversary and homecoming, women or men's days. The goal is to make them a part of the activities of the church.

Visiting the Hospitalized

Purpose: your task as pastor is to be a part of the healing team. You go to minister unto the total person. No person on the hospital staff has the full responsibility of dealing with the hospitalized member at all levels: body, mind, soul, and will.

Methods: (What the pastor should do)

1. Make a pastoral visit to hospitalized members.

It is your responsibility as pastor to care for the sick among the flock. The ministerial staff, deacons and other members can help supplement your hospital ministry but none can substitute for you.

2. Make the visit as soon as you know of the member's hospitalization.

This should be done within a day or two. Your presence, the awareness that you know and care, is a part of the healing process.

3. Check with a nurse or knock lightly before entering a sick room.

You are the pastor of the flock, not the chief administrator of the hospital. This will help in preventing you and your member embarrassment.

4. Be serious-minded but not rigid. Be warm but not overly humorous. Keep your personal identity clear, that you are the pastor. Sickness and hospitalization are serious, and you should treat it as such.

5. Do not attempt to diagnose or identify with the member's condition.

You are the pastor, not the medical doctor. You do not know what the condition is, nor do you know how they got that way. Jesus did not ask the blind man how he lost his sight, nor did Jesus say, "I know what it is like to be blind." Jesus opened his eyes that he might see.

6. Be dressed appropriately as a pastor (preferably tie and coat).

Your personal appearance has much to do with your member acknowledging you as pastor. The nurses do not wear just anything; the surgeon has specific dress, and so should the pastor.

7. Have a word of prayer and Scripture reading.

You have to be sensitive in this area. You should not automatically conclude that you are going to pray each time you visit a hospitalized member. There are situations when your prayer will be interpreted that you believe the members are dying, and you will not see them again, or it will be interpreted to mean that you believe the member is very seriously ill. The Holy Spirit will lead you in this matter.

Methods: (What the pastor should *not* do)

1. Send someone else as his representative.

There will be times when you will be physically unable to make the visit. Even then you should attempt to contact the member by phone or card.

2. Stay too long when visiting.

Your presence is what is important, not the longevity of your stay.

3. Talk of the wrath of God or project the idea that sickness comes about as a result of personal sin committed.

This is not the time or the place to make members feel or think guilt-ridden thoughts about their condition. You have to admit you do not know why this member is sick at this particular time with this particular illness.

4. Ask "What is wrong?"

It is none of your business. You come not to find out what is wrong but to declare what is right.

5. Sit on the side of the bed.

The hospital bed is private.

6. Do not smoke while visiting.

You are there to minister unto the person, not to socialize with them.

7. Give them tokens (such as money, cards, candy, flowers, etc., unless done consistently with all hospitalized members).

One sure way to offend members is to play favorites. Treat all as one.

8. Tell the hospitalized member when you are coming back to visit and then not do it.

A hospitalized member has nothing to do but to wait on your return.

Visiting in a Correctional Institution

Purpose: I was in prison, and ye came unto me (Matt. 25:36, KJV).

In obedience to the command of our Christ we must make pastoral visits to persons incarcerated. We go as pastors, not as lawyers or legal consultants. As we go we bring the power of the gospel to bear upon the situation that by grace, through faith, we who were aliens and strangers can be made right through the redemptive work of Jesus Christ.

Methods:
1. Visit the incarcerated person. Do not remove the right hand of fellowship from a member who has either been accused or convicted of a wrong.

2. Visit the family of the incarcerated member. Pastoral care is needed to the family because of the "lost." There is a physical loss and perhaps a financial loss.

3. When making the visit, go not as a lawyer, bail bondsman, legal counselor, or judge: go as a pastor. There will be times when a member wants your advice. Give it as a pastor. Never tell a person what you would do if in their place. You are not, so you cannot tell them.

4. Establish a pastoral relationship. Your presence, care, and concern will enhance the development of this relationship. Tell the member why you have come and what you hope to do. You are not there to be used or misused.

5. Do not make promises or tell an institutionalized person you are going to do something and then not do it. You must understand that a person incarcerated has nothing but time to think, time to wait, and

time to expect. Your failure to come through will diminish your creditability.

6. As a pastor you can work in a supplementary role. Work with the lawyer or help obtain one, be a character witness (if you can honestly be one), write reference letters, make telephone calls, be an intercessor between the incarcerated person and their family.

7. Pray for the redemption of the member. You go not just to "see" the member but to minister. Wrong can be made right, sin can be forgiven, and mercy can be received with justice.

Visiting in a Mental Institution

Purpose: "He asked him, what is thy name? And he answered, saying, My name is Legion: for we are many" (Mark 5:9, KJV). The objective of this pastoral ministry is to bring the healing power of Christ upon mentally disturbed persons and their families.

Methods:
1. Check with a staff person before making the visit. You are the pastor, not the administrator of the mental institution. The staff person can assist you by telling you the members' present condition, their progress, specific needs and problems, and how you can be of the greatest help to the member.

2. Go as pastor, not as psychoanalyst or psychologist. You should be informed of mental disorders and mental dysfunctions, but this is for your own awareness, not to be used by you as clinical technician.

3. Do not be apprehensive or show your anxiety. You cannot help a person you are afraid of, and you will not reach a person unless you are able to "touch" them.

4. Affirm the patient where you can. Never argue, even if you think their thinking is wrong or in error. You have to be sensitive to the fact that you are ministering unto a person that does not have full rational power.

5. You should be at your best mental health before visiting a mental patient. You should have a word of prayer, think your thoughts clear, do not be anxious or in a hurry when you go to visit.

6. The use of silence can be therapeutic. "God came to Laban the

Syrian in a dream by night, and said unto him, Take heed that thou speak not to Jacob either good or bad" (Gen. 31:24, KJV). We do not have to speak in every situation. The silence can speak for us.

7. Be prepared for confessions. Oftentimes mental patients have guilt feelings or anxieties that they need to deal with in a confessional way. Listen to their confessions, affirming that through Jesus Christ, they can and will be forgiven.

8. Do not try to identify with the patients by telling them you have had the same thoughts or the same feelings or experiences. You have to be sensitive in this area. This can lead the patient into believing that they are well when they are sick. You do have to identify with the patient at the person level.

9. Have a word of prayer. The language of prayer can speak to the heart as well as to the head.

For the pastor to be an effective minister of healing he must have a holistic view of persons. No dissecting persons. The whole person must be made whole.

The attributes of compassion and sensitivity will enhance his functioning ability as he seeks to serve his people. The pastor will only reach people that he 'sees' as standing in need of God's grace.

The way to reach people is through the ministry of touch. To do this the pastor must have an incarnational model. He must be real flesh and blood where the people are. If his people are in the hospital, convalescent home, jails and prisons, mental institutions and shut-in rooms, the pastor must be there, caring for the flock which the Holy Spirit has made him overseer.

The ministry of visitation must be kept in its broader context of caring for the other. We must not narrow visiting down to just going over to "see" the person, but rather, we must go to minister and care for the person.

Jesus is our example in this pastoral model. He healed the sick, opened blinded eyes, unstopped deaf ears, called demons out of the mentally deranged, and straightened out withered hands.

Our task as pastors is to emulate Jesus in the ministry of healing.

5

The Pastor as Priest

Thou shalt put upon Aaron the holy garments, and anoint him, and sanctify him; that he may minister unto me in the priest's office (Ex. 40:13, KJV).

AN OVERVIEW OF THE PRIESTHOOD

In Israel, the priesthood represented the nation's relationship with God. The original intention in the Mosaic covenant was for the entire nation to be a kingdom of priests (Ex. 19:6; Lev. 11:44 ff.; Num. 15:40). The covenant of God was mediated through the priesthood. In biblical theology the concepts of priesthood and covenant are closely related. Because of the covenant at Sinai, Israel was meant to be "a kingdom of priests and a holy nation" (Ex. 19:6). God's holy character was to be reflected in the life of Israel (Lev. 11:44 ff.; Num. 15:40). The fact that God vested priestly functions in one tribe did not release the rest of the nation from their original obligation.[1]

When the priests ministered, they did so as the representatives of the people. It was a practical necessity that the corporate obligation of the covenant people should be carried out by priestly representatives. Furthermore, the priests, in their separated condition, symbolized the purity and holiness God required. They were a visible reminder of God's righteous requirements. The primary function of the Levitical priesthood, therefore, was to maintain and assure, as well as re-establish, the holiness of the chosen people of God (Ex. 28:38; Lev. 10:7; Num. 18:1).[2]

In early Israel, an important function of priests was to discover the will of God by means of the ephod (1 Sam. 23:6-12). They were

133

constantly occupied with instruction in the law (Mal. 2:4-7). Of course, their duties always included offering of sacrifices. Early priests were guardians of the sanctuary and interpreters of the oracle (1 Sam. 14:18). Instructions in the law belonged to the priests (Hos. 4:1-10). The priest acted as judge, a consequence of his imparting answers to legal questions (Ex. 18:7-16).

THREEFOLD DIVISION OF PRIESTS

The priesthood was divided into three groups: (1) the high priest, (2) ordinary priests, and (3) Levites. All three descended from Levi. All priests were Levites, but by no means were all Levites priests. The lowest order of priesthood was the Levite who cared for the service of the sanctuary.[3]

The essential function of the Levitical priesthood is to assure, maintain, and constantly reestablish the holiness of the elect people of God (Ex. 28:38; Num. 18:1).[4] They are responsible for the care of the courts and chambers of the sanctuary, the cleansing of the sacred vessels, the preparation of the cereal of offerings, and the service of praise (1 Chron. 23:28-32). Some are mentioned particularly as being porters or gatekeepers (1 Chron. 9:19; 26:1,19), some as treasurers (1 Chron. 26:20), and some as choristers and musicians (Ezra 3:10; Neh. 12:27; 2 Chron. 8:14). The Levites also have a teaching function as interpreters of the law (Neh. 8:7-9; 2 Chron. 17:7-9; 35:3). Levites assist the priest in administration of justice (1 Chron. 23:4; 26:29) and in the charge of the treasury (Ezra 8:33-34).[4]

The high priest represented the highest level of priesthood. He represented bodily the height of the purity of the priesthood. He bore the names of all the tribes of Israel on his breastplate into the sanctuary, thus representing all the people before God (Ex. 28:29). Only he could enter the holiest of all and only on one day a year to make expiation for the sins of the entire nation.

The ordinary priests were the cultic specialists. They were restricted to the Levitical house of Aaron (Ex. 28:1,41; 29:9; Num. 18:7) and must be free from physical defects (Lev. 21:16-23).

The chief functions of the postexilic priesthood are the care of the vessels of the sanctuary and the sacrificial duties of the altar: only the priest may sacrifice (Num. 18:5-7). The priesthood also retained its ancient prerogative of giving instruction in the ways and requirements of God (Mal. 2:6-7; Jer. 18:18).

The priests are the custodians of medical lore and so play an important part in safeguarding the health of the community (Lev. 13—15). They retain their traditional role of administrators of justice (Deut. 17:8-9; 21:5; 2 Chron. 19:8-11; Ezek. 44:24). Finally, it is the priests who are responsible for blowing the trumpets which summon the people for war or for the keeping of a feast (Num. 10:1-10; 31:6), and they alone may bless in the name of God (Num. 6:22-27).[5]

THE PASTOR'S PRIESTLY MINISTRIES

Worship Leader

The pastor is the worship leader of the congregation. As he seeks to shepherd the flock, he must lead his people to the Good Shepherd.

To have an effective ministry in this area, the pastor needs to have an understanding of worship.

The word *worship* comes from an Anglo-Saxon word *weorthscipe*—"worth" and "ship"—meaning one worthy of reverence and honor. When we worship we are declaring God's worth.[6]

To worship we must know that the Lord, he is God. We give our reverence, our respect, our repentant selves to him. The Lord is God over us. He is transcendent, above and beyond us, and yet the Lord our God is immanent, near and with us. We praise him and worship him because of who he is: God, and beside him there is no other.

To worship we acknowledge who we are. We are the sheep of his pasture. We are not little shepherds guiding ourselves, feeding ourselves, protecting ourselves, but rather we are the sheep of God's pasture. As sheep we are in a dilemma because we do not know which way to go. We do not know where to find food or water for the emptiness of our lives, but as sheep of God's pasture we have the blessed assurance that he will lead us into green pastures and lead us beside still waters.

To worship is to accept the lordship of Christ. We ask the Lord to both come into our lives and take up residence, and we also ask him to take over our lives and have precedence.

We know that as we are, we are inadequate and insufficient; but we know a Great Savior who feeds us when we are hungry and finds us when we are lost.

To worship affirms the goodness of God in our lives. We can say with assurance, the Lord is good, his mercy is everlasting, and his truth endures to all generations.

There is much confusion and chaos in this world; there is much hurt and hopelessness. We do not turn our backs or stick our heads into the sand to these awesome realities, but we can through God's grace and his continual presence with us affirm that he is good.

The Psychology of Worship

It is most important for the black pastor to have a sensitivity and an understanding of the attitude of his people as they assemble themselves for worship.

The attitude of black people when they come to worship is one which is molded from oppression and depression. There is a peculiar sense of frustration and failure in their lives. They are frustrated because they see where they want to go, yet they realize where they are. They have a sense of failure not because they have not achieved, but because they have had to excel their white counterpart just to get in the waiting line.

When black people assemble for worship they not only want, but they need release. They have to express themselves in ways that will give vent to their pent up emotions. For a few moments, usually about two hours, they have to express themselves freely, without all of the societal restraints.

Black people have gone through an identity crisis, both with themselves and in the larger community. They have always known who they are and for the most part whose they are, but there were many negative influences which sought to distort their personal image.

When they assemble for worship they want to know that they are a child of the king and that the Lord is on their side.

As the black pastor leads the worship service he must keep in mind the threefold dimension of the worshipers perspective.

There is the recollection of the past. This is remembering that the Lord has brought us from a mighty long way. It is not an attempt to forget from whence we have come or how we have come. It is fully realizing and recalling that it has been by the ever present and guiding hand of our God that we have been safe this far by faith.

We can hear this expressed in our worship tradition of testimony, "When I think about how good God has been," "If it had not been for the Lord, I would not have made it." Both of these are expressions of God's providential and perpetual care in leading his people into their Promised Lands.

Secondly, there is the affirmation of the present. "The Lord is blessing me right now." It matters not how hard or harsh my present conditions may be, for I have the awareness and the assurance that the Lord is ever with me and I am daily, presently, a recipient of his "now" blessings. This understanding and sensitivity to the affirmation of the present needs to be strongly stressed because many persons have erroneously concluded that black worship is simply otherworldly directed. This is quite false. I have the expectation and hope for the future knowing that it is going to be better because I have the assurance right now of what the Lord is doing.

Thirdly, there is the eschatological hope. This "end time" hope is based upon "now time" goodness. We hear it expressed in the black worship tradition, "Just as soon as my feet strike Zion, I am going to lay down my heavy burdens." This hopeful expression is based upon the nowness and nearness of God through Christ being a heavy-load carrier and a burden bearer.

"I'm going to fly away," because running is already in my feet and clapping is in my hands. My eye is on the star post in glory, and my mind is on heaven.

When black people assemble for worship, the pastor, as worship leader, must keep these dimensions in perspective.

The Pastor's Preparation for Worship

You, as pastor, must enter the secret closet and there pray to the Father, that he may "reward thee openly" (Matt. 6:6, KJV).

You have to spend some time with God if you are going to speak for

God and stand in his holy sanctuary before his people.

The people of God who assemble for worship will for the most part come just as they are. You as worship leader cannot come that way. Too often the people are out of line with God's ways and will, and the pastor is out of touch in communicating what the Lord would have him to say at that particular time.

If the pastor is to go ahead and prepare the way for the Lord's coming, he must be prepared to lead the worship experience.

Physical Preparation

We have the treasure in an earthen vessel that the excellency of the power may be of God and not of ourselves (2 Cor. 4:7). If we are to receive the treasure, we need to have the earthen vessel in the best possible shape.

Rest and sleep are essential. You will not be effective during the worship services if you are tired or worn. Your people will come this way: weary, worn, and sad; but they will not be lifted if their pastor is in the same situation as they are. The only thing two tired people can do together is lean on each other, without either one being able to lift the other.

Bodily conditioning is necessary. You do not have to be in such physical condition to compete in the Olympics, but you should have enough physical stamina and vitality to lead the worship.

Sitting, standing, praying, singing, preaching, listening, feeling, and speaking are all quite exhaustive in and of themselves. When you combine all of these together at one particular time for approximately a two-hour duration, you have used quite a bit of energy.

Just being in the presence of a large congregation is in itself draining.

To enhance bodily conditioning, the pastor should develop a routine schedule of body exercise that is conducive to his body build, age, previous medical history, and present physical condition.

This may take the form of walking, jogging, swimming, cycling or some exercise that will enable him to use his muscles so that both heart and lungs are exerted.

Spiritual Preparation

When Moses came down from Mount Sinai, he glowed, having come from the presence of God. When we come into the pulpit and sanctuary to lead the worship, we ought to come "glowing."

To do this we must maintain an active prayer life. You cannot speak *for* God if you are not *on* speaking terms with him yourself.

Meditation and reflection will help equip you to lead the worship. In God's law, his rule, his way, meditate day and night (Ps. 1:2).

Do not attempt to speak to the people until the Lord has spoken to you. So often we know what we want to say, but it may not be what the Lord wants us to say.

Find some quiet place to sit still and listen to hear what the Lord is saying to you. Learn to pray by leaving the prayer channel open. We close our prayers by saying amen as if to be saying, OK, Lord, that is all that I had to say, without giving the Lord an opportunity to talk back.

Repentance and Confession

Isaiah was only ready to go forth to speak for the Lord after he confessed that he was a man of unclean lips (Isa. 6:5). We cannot go forth to call our people unto repentance and demand of them to make confessions when we ourselves are arrested in our own sins. We must ask the Lord to purge us, so that he might use us in his service.

Emotional Tuning and Sensitivity

As we go to lead the worship we must be in touch with our own emotions. If we are at a spiritual low ourselves, we must not attempt to go to the sanctuary appearing to be on a spiritual high. That is deceitful and detrimental to the worship experience. Jesus has told us that we must worship in spirit and in truth (John 4:24).

Our lowness, if lovingly and redemptively shared, can be the contact point of reaching and lifting our people. Deep can call unto deep until low valleys are made high mountains.

The Order of Service

"Let all things be done decently and in order" (1 Cor. 14:40, KJV).

The order of service should not be haphazardly thrown together or ritualistically done.

There are three basic factors that ought to be used as the criteria for what components are to be used as well as those that should not be used.

The worship service must be Christ centered, biblically based, and people oriented.

Using this threefold check list, each component of the worship can be scrutinized as to its needfulness and purpose in the worship service.

An Analysis of an Order of Worship

I am aware that within the black worship tradition there is no one set order of worship. The worship style will vary with the pastor's preference, congregational receptiveness, cultural conditioning, and socioeconomical factors. What I hope to put forth is an analysis of the rationale as to why what is being done within a "typical" black worship setting.

Devotions: At a time when usually the deacons or other worship leaders begin the worship experience by calling the worshipers' attention from the world and themselves to devote their attention Godward.

Prelude: Usually an organ meditation setting the atmosphere for the approach of the worship leaders. (I say "leaders" with the understanding that in the black worship tradition, the congregation are the real leaders and participants.)

Call to Worship: When the pastor or associate minister announces the presence of the Lord in his holy temple.

Processional: The coming in of the pastor, minister of music, choir, and other worship directors.

Congregational or Opening Hymn: When both the congregation and choir rise to sing together. The purpose is for the creation of the community of fellowship.

Old Testament Scriptures: The reading out loud of the Old Testament Scriptures, either with the minister reading or the congregation together.

Prayer: This is usually a morning prayer, led by a deacon, associate minister, or sometimes the pastor. The prayer is usually one of thanksgiving and a petition for the presence of the Lord to be with his people.

Music: The choir(s) will render selections usually of a variety. Some churches have older choirs who do anthems and spirituals, while younger choirs do hymns and gospels.

Recognition of Visitors: There are very few black churches where a visitor can go that one will not be made welcome.

Pastoral Emphasis Announcements: The black church is the communicator and preserver of information in the black community. Announcements concerning the congregation and the community are given. The pastor will come to give special encouragement or direction pertaining to the congregation's actions.

Offering: Most essential in the black worship experience. Even persons who have nothing to give will be prayed for as though they did give. Tithes and offerings are the practical ideal, but there is much diversity in the names of numerous offerings.

Music: The instrumental playing and choral singing are vital in setting the mood and tempo of the worship experience. Usually the music at this point of the worship is celebrative and up tempo in nature.

New Testament Scriptures: The biblical reading is essential in validating the worship experience.

Pastoral Prayer or Altar Call: This is the high priestly prayer for the congregation. A time when the pastor as priest takes the concerns of the people before the throne of God. He may invite worshipers to come forward for personal emphasis. When black people ask their pastor to "pray for me," they mean it.

Sermon: The climactic moment in the worship experience. A time when all assembled will hear the word from heaven. The pastor is expected to preach, making the Word "live" for his people.

Invitation to Christian Discipleship: The expression will be heard, "the doors of the church are now open." This does not mean it is time to leave, but rather a time to come and make a profession of faith in Jesus Christ.

Benediction: Not necessarily a closing of the worship experience, but an affirming of all that has happened and a prayer that the Lord's presence will be with his people even as they leave his sanctuary. The benediction is a hopeful anticipation that we will meet again in this life and heavenly expectation if we do not.

Postlude: The "afterglow" of the worship experience. Even after the sun has set, there is an afterglow of the warmth and radiance that it leaves behind.

Recessional: The pastor and choirs will recess out of the sanctuary.

Usually the pastor will station himself in a place where he can receive and greet his members.

Worship Assistants

The pastor is understood to be the worship leader. He must not, however, appear or become the master of ceremonies for the worship.

He leads the worship experience by being led himself. He must never feel that he has to subscribe to a fixed liturgical order, or he cannot be open to the Spirits direction. If he leads as he is lead, all of the worshipers will experience the Lord's presence among his people.

To assist the pastor as worship leader, there are several persons and factors which need to be considered as vitally important to enhance the worship experience.

1. *The Associate Ministers:* If the associate ministers are to participate in leading the worship, they should be prepared for such before entering the pulpit. Scripture selections should be made, who will pray, who will assist in receiving the offering, who will announce congregational hymns, or whatever else will be needed to make the worship experience what it should be.

2. *The Deacons:* The deacons should come to the sanctuary together to lead the devotional service. They should not coincidentally pop in. They should have arranged who will sing at least the first song and who will lead the first prayer. If they are going to invite the congregation to pray, sing or testify, this should be made known at the start of the devotional service. Scripture selections, responsive readings, songs, a word of testimony, or whatever is to be done should have some order and preparation to it. The deacons should know who will assist in receiving the offering, who will pray, and who will assist during the invitation.

3. *The Minister of Music:* The minister of music must see him/herself as having a ministry through musical expression. The minister of music, through his/her skills, knowledge of the psychology of worship, sensitivity to the pastor, choir and congregation can make the worship experience a blessing or a burden for the pastor.

The pastor must coordinate, correlate, and communicate with the minister of music and vice versa. The congregation will suffer drastically if the pastor and minister of music are not functioning as a team.

The minister of music has a fivefold responsibility during the worship experience.

He/she is responsible to the Lord.

He/she is responsible to the pastor.

He/she is responsible to the congregation.

He/she is responsible to the music department.

He/she is responsible to themselves.

4. *The Ushers:* The ushers are more than standing decoration during the worship experience. They invite and introduce. They invite the worshipers to come into the Lord's sanctuary and introduce them to the Lord's presence by seating them in his midst.

The pastor must work with the ushers as to when to open the doors, when to seat worshipers, how and when to receive the offering, how to arrange special seating in the pulpit and choir area, how to receive visitors, especially guest ministers, and how to be aware of the needs and direction from the pulpit.

As the pastor leads the worship experience, he must be lead by the Holy Spirit as to what to say and do and when to say and do it.

He must have congregational sensitivity and an awareness of the psychology of worship. The pastor or worship leader is not a one-man performer, but he must see himself as the conductor of the orchestra, where each member has a part to play and has something to say even if it is no more than saying amen.

The associate ministers, deacons, minister of music, and ushers must be harmonized into a team concept, working together for the good of the flock of God.

MINISTERING AT BAPTISMS

The pastor should have a biblical bases and understanding of the meaning and purpose of Christian baptism before he can administer this command of Christ.

The word *baptism* comes from the Greek word *baptizo*, which means to dip repeatedly, to immerse or submerge.

In the New Testament, *baptizo* is used in several ways: to cleanse by dipping or submerging oneself in water (Mark 7:4); to wash hands by submerging them in water (Luke 11:38); to be overwhelmed or submerged in calamities or cares (Matt. 20:22-23; Mark 10:38-39). But the principal use of the word in the New Testament is in reference to the ordinance of baptism.[7]

The word *baptism* refers to the act of being baptized or immersed and is used only four times (Mark 7:4,8; Heb. 6:2; 9:10) where it refers to the Jewish ceremonial cleansing. The word *baptisma* denotes the significance or meaning involved in the act of baptism. It appears twenty-two times in the New Testament.[8]

Baptism is to be administered to those who have experienced an inward change by a conscious acceptance of Jesus as Savior (Acts 16:31-33). John the Baptist refused baptism to the Sadducees and Pharisees who knew no repentance (Matt. 3:7-9). Peter demanded repentance as the basis for baptism (Acts 2:38). Acts 2:41 (KJV) says, "They that gladly received his word were baptized." Paul baptized the Philippian jailer after he had believed on the Lord Jesus Christ and was saved (Acts 16:30-33). While baptism is not necessary for salvation, it is an act of obedience (Matt. 28:19) by which we show that our faith for salvation is in the death, burial, and resurrection of Jesus Christ and that we have died to sin; the old life has been buried, and we are raised to a new life in Christ.[9] "Know ye not, that so many of us as were baptized into Jesus Christ were baptized into his death? Therefore we are buried with him by baptism into death: that like as Christ was raised up from the dead by the glory of the father, even so we also should walk in newness of life" (Rom. 6:3-4, KJV).

In concluding, Christian baptism is immersion: death, submersion—burial, and emerging—resurrection. Baptism is no symbol, for it is based upon faith, repentance, obedience, submission, and a life commitment.

Pastoral Preparation for the Baptismal Service

The baptismal service should be planned with care and the utmost consideration. It should not be randomly put together or simply conveniently done.

The pastor should pray for guidance and for cleansing as he is about to participate in one of the highest priestly offices in carrying out the command of Christ.

It is the pastor's task to assign designated persons to prepare the baptistry.

The dressing rooms for the brothers and sisters to be baptized should be available and clean.

There should be members assigned to assist in the preparation of the baptismal candidate(s).

The pastor should be properly attired for this most sacred moment. His robe should be fresh and pressed, and his boots, sleeves, or other garments should look the part.

It is important for the pastor, through preaching and teaching, to help the congregation understand and appreciate the major significance of what is happening during the baptismal service.

The pastor has to instruct the associate ministers, minister of music, deacons, ushers, and other worship leaders of the direction he wants the baptismal service to follow.

The minister of music or choir director plays a vital role in setting the tone and creating the atmosphere that will enhance the baptismal service.

If the pastor will need assistance in the actual baptizing service, he should secure such in plenty of time.

The pastor should give last minute encouragement and instruction to the candidates before leading them to the baptizing.

Congregational Preparation for the Baptismal Service

Baptism is a public, not a private, act. It is personal, but it is done within the community of other baptized believers. As such the congregation participates in the baptismal service with the candidates being baptized.

Each baptismal service is a time of renewal and rededication for each baptized member. It is a time of examination of their commitment to Christ and followship to his commands.

The baptismal service is also an evangelistic service in that it seeks through demonstration to reach and win others for Christ. When John the Baptist was baptizing in the Jordan, multitudes came to him, asking, "What then shall we do?" John answered that they should be baptized for the remission of their sin and "Bear fruits that befit repentance" (Luke 3:7-10).

The baptismal service is a time of Christian community solidarity. There are many things within a local congregation that tend to divide and separate us into groupings, that is, age difference, personality traits, personal preference in serving in the church, and so forth; but the baptismal service is a time when the whole church community can come together and be as one.

What the congregation can and needs to do to be prepared for a baptismal service is:

1. Assemble at the designated time and place for the baptismal service. As has been stated, the baptismal service is not a private or individualistic act, but is one in which the church community shares and participates.

2. Have a biblical understanding of the meaning and purpose of baptism. This will be the pastor's responsibility in shepherding the sheep in this area.

3. Come together in the spirit of worship for the baptismal service. Nothing will hinder and even prevent a baptismal service from being what it ought to be any quicker than a congregation that has assembled for everything but to share in the baptismal service.

4. Seek to bring the newly baptized member into the fellowship circle of the church. In each church there is the membership circle which one joins by fulfilling the membership responsibilities. But there also is the fellowship circle to which the members have to open the door to let the new person become a part of the Christian community. It is the congregation's responsibility to seek the member at the fellowship level and not wait for the member to seek them.

5. Pray for the newly baptized member. The words of Paul to the church at Thessalonica are most applicable in this context, "Brethren, pray for us" (1 Thess. 5:25). Pray that the new member will grow in wisdom, knowledge, and understanding of what it means to be a disciple of Christ. Pray that the church family will embrace the brother or sister in the spirit of Christian fellowship. Pray that through the new

member's baptism others may come to accept Jesus Christ as their Lord and Savior. Pray for yourself to be strengthened in the Christian way that your life will be a help and not a hindrance, a blessing and not a burden, for the newly baptized member.

The Candidates' Preparation for the Baptismal Service

As Philip was led by the Spirit to go down to the road which led from Jerusalem to Gaza, he met the Ethiopian eunuch. After preaching the gospel and illuminating his mind about the Scripture text he was reading, the eunuch wanted to know, "What is to prevent my being baptized?" (Acts 8:26-39).

The candidate should have all "hindrances" removed prior to the baptismal service.

Spiritual Preparation

The person needs to have repented—that is, a turning from sin and self toward the Savior. The candidate must be converted. Jesus' words still must be heard and obediently followed. You must be born again. The candidate must believe, by accepting Jesus as Savior and as Lord over his or her life. The candidate must make a confession of faith. The Scripture teaches that if you believe in your heart and confess with your mouth Jesus is Lord, you shall be saved (Rom. 10:9).

Some instruction should be given prior to the baptismal service. The pastor and local congregation will need to work this out.

The instruction should include at least the meaning and purpose of baptism, the responsibilities of the baptized believers and the member, and church's responsibility to each other.

Physical Preparation

The baptismal candidate should be properly informed of the time and place of the baptismal service. Family and friends will no doubt want to be informed of such so as to witness such a glorious occasion.

The proper clothes should be worn. Usually white baptismal robes or white shirts and trousers. The baptismal service is not a time for the candidates to demonstrate their stylishness or their wardrobes.

The approach and method of baptism should be fully explained. The baptismal candidates should be told just what will happen once they are in the water. If they will be led into one side and out the other, this should be explained. If a stool or another person will assist the pastor, this should be made known.

After the member has been baptized, a proper place should be provided to dress, and someone should be there to assist. The newly baptized members should not be forsaken after they have been baptized but rather should be embraced.

The new members should be informed when the new member orientation will be held and what their responsibilities are in this area.

Postbaptismal Ministry

Jesus said, "Come unto me, . . . and learn of me" (Matt. 11:28-30, KJV).

As a pastor you cannot afford to dip (baptize) members and then leave them to "drip dry." We have the responsibility to teach the new member to observe all things whatsoever the Lord has commanded of us to do.

To develop the postbaptismal ministry there should be a New Member's Class. A specialized ministry designed and developed for the new member.

Just how extensive and in-depth you will want to go will be determined by your congregational needs and your ministerial training.

There would be four general areas that I believe ought to be included in any new member orientation. They are: biblical understanding, Christian doctrine or the teaching of Christ, church ordinances, and church history.

By biblical understanding, I do not mean attempt to teach the whole Bible, but inform the new member what the Bible is, the purpose of Scriptures, the organizational structure, how to read and study the Bible.

You cannot teach Christian doctrine in one session or in several sessions for that matter, but you can begin to inform the new member of what Jesus has taught and commanded of us through his Word.

The church ordinances are, namely, the Lord's Supper and

baptism. The members must be told of their responsibility to the church and the church's responsibility to the member. The fourth area would be church history. The new members should have some understanding as to why they are a part of a particular denominational persuasion.

An "older" member who is mature in the faith should be assigned to each new member, to help the pastor in caring for and shepherding the new member. Periodically the pastor should present all new members to the congregation, and he should have some system where he can contact and begin to know on a personal-pastoral basis all new members.

MINISTERING AT THE LORD'S SUPPER

"This do in remembrance of me" (1 Cor. 11:24, KJV).

As the pastor seeks to minister at the Lord's Supper he needs a biblical understanding of whose supper it is, who may receive it, and how it is to be observed.

The Lord's Supper is a remembrance of Jesus Christ: covenant, communion, lordship of Christ, eschatological hope, and proclamation.

The Lord's Supper as a Covenant

In each of the four basic accounts of the Lord's Supper, stress is given to the covenant (Mark 14:24; Matt. 26:28) or the new covenant (Luke 22:20; 1 Cor. 11:25) set forth in his blood. The word *covenant* is to be used with the understanding not as a contract to be negotiated and then agreement made but as acceptance of the will or the offer of God through Jesus Christ. The idea is never that of an agreement negotiated between God and man. God has not invited man to meet him at a "summit conference" to work out some mutually acceptable agreements. God remains sovereign in his covenants; he alone determines the conditions, and he alone guarantees their validity.[10]

When Jesus is quoted as saying "This cup is the new covenant in my blood" (1 Cor. 11:25), his reference is to God's own provision for man's proper relationship to himself and to life.

By the way of the cross, man is reconciled to God. The "blood"—

the life given—is the true and living way. The blood of Jesus, his life given, is the pledge of assurance of the kingdom of God (Mark 14:25; Matt. 26:29). Among other things, the cup of the Lord's Supper outwardly attests to God's new covenant, made secure in the triumphant death of Jesus Christ.[11]

The Lord's Supper as Sacrifice

The idea of sacrifice is implied in Mark 14:24 (Matt. 26:28); but in 1 Corinthians 11:25 ("This cup is the new covenant in my blood.") and in Luke 22:20 ("This cup which is poured out for you is the new covenant in my blood."), Jesus himself is the sacrifice. He gives himself. This is the ultimate of the prophetic understanding of true sacrifice as that of self-giving rather than the offering of an animal.

The Lord's Supper proclaims the fulfillment of this covenant in Jesus' giving of his blood (that is, his life, himself) "for many" (Mark 14:24; Matt. 26:28) or "for you" (1 Cor. 11:24; Luke 22:20). The Lord's Supper affirms a covenant in which the Lord and his disciples, Savior and those being saved, give themselves in loving sacrifice.[12]

The Lord's Supper as Remembrance

The command to repeat the supper "in remembrance" of Jesus is found in 1 Corinthians 11:24-25 and Luke 22:19. The Lord's Supper is a "memorial" in the sense that it looks back in grateful memory to Golgotha, but it is more. It is remembrance of Jesus Christ, not dead but alive and present in his body, the church. Embodied in his church, he is redeeming it by drawing it into his kind of existence and life by first drawing it into his kind of sacrifice, not cultic but self-denying and self-giving (Mark 10:38; John 12:24; Rom. 6:3-11; Gal. 2:20; 2 Cor. 5:15).[13]

The Lord's Supper as Communion

Paul is explicit and emphatic in holding the cup and loaf to be "the communion (*koinōnia*) of the blood of Christ" and "the communion of the body of Christ" (1 Cor. 10:16, KJV). The breakdown in fellowship in Corinth accounts for the major stress given this aspect of the Lord's Supper. Participation in the blood (life given) and body (the body of Christ, the church) belongs properly to covenant and sacrifice as well as to the idea of the eschatological banquet of which the Lord's Supper is an anticipation.

Communion *(koinōnia)* "with the Father and with His Son Jesus Christ" and with one another belongs essentially to the Christian life (1 John 1:1-4), and it is one function of the Lord's Supper to express and cultivate this communion. Christ is not embodied in the bread or the cup, and his living presence is not limited to the observance of the supper, but it is not the Lord's Supper unless he is present in the fellowship of his people.[14]

The Lord's Supper as Eschatological Hope

Jesus looked forward to drinking the fruit of the vine "new" (Mark 14:25) or "new with you [his disciples]" (Matt. 26:29) in the kingdom of God (Mark) or of his Father (Matthew) or "until the kingdom of God comes" (Luke 22:18). Paul saw the supper as proclamation of the death of the Lord, until he comes (1 Cor. 11:26). *Maranatha* (Lord come!) was probably a prayer in Aramaic uttered in connection with the supper, as well as at other times. The supper does look forward as well as backward and to the present.[15]

The Lord's Supper as Symbol and Reality

Cup and loaf are symbols, but symbols presuppose something symbolized. Although symbols are employed the Lord's Supper, if genuine, is more than symbolism. Remembering, giving thanks, worship, being called to obedience to Christ the Lord, enjoying the presence of Christ embodied in his church, proclamation of Christ's death, and the affirmation of an eschatological hope are far more than symbols. The Lord's Supper is not magic, of itself imparting grace. On the other hand, if it is mere symbol it becomes an empty, cultic practice. What belongs to genuine observance of the Lord's Supper is not restricted to the supper, but it belongs to the purpose of the supper to cultivate and give expression to memory, worship, obedience, communion, continuing sacrifice, and hope.[16]

The Pastor at the Lord's Table

"When the hour came, he [Jesus] sat at table, and the apostles with him" (Luke 22:14).

The first concern of the pastor in administering the Lord's Supper is preparation. In Luke 22:7-13, Jesus gave specific instructions to Peter and John to go into Jerusalem, and there they would meet a man carrying a jar of water. He would lead them to a furnished upper room where Jesus would eat the Passover meal with his disciples.

The man, the upper room, the food for the meal, and the time of usage had already been secured by Jesus. The pastor, as the shepherd of the flock, must also make adequate preparation for the observance of the Lord's Supper. The Lord's Supper should not be haphazardly put together or placed at the end of another worship service from a lack of concern. The Lord's Supper is a special service in and of itself and should be administered and observed as such.

The pastor has the responsibility of arranging the Lord's Supper and of announcing it in plenty of time to the congregation. The arrangement concerns are making sure the Lord's Supper table is properly set. The bread and wine should be placed on the table and arranged with reverence and respect as to what the major significance is of what they represent.

Table linens, napkins, gloves, cups, and trays should all be presentable for this most sacred time of usage.

The pastor should work closely with the minister of music or choir director in arranging the musical selections and the musicians in what selections will be played for mood and atmosphere. The Lord's Supper time is not the time for the pastor to randomly pick musical selections, nor is it a time for the minister of music or choir director to wonder what they are going to sing or play once the service has started.

The pastor has the further responsibility in preparing the deacons, who are to assist him. Nothing will kill the reverence of the Lord's

Supper any quicker than deacons or others who are to assist not knowing what they are to do.

The day before or maybe even a week before the pastor may need to go over the order of service, the plan for serving the congregation, how empty cups will be collected, how the trays will be passed, who will assist at the table, and so forth. Once again I must state, the Lord's Supper is not time for on-the-job training. That training should already have taken place.

The second concern in administering the Lord's Supper is penitence. The pastor should have genuine realization of his own sin and godly sorrow for wrongdoings. I do not mean to pray or say in a general way "Forgive me of my sin," for that is almost like praying "Forgive me for existing." What the pastor needs to do is have a moment of self-examination, confessing his faults to his Father who hears and sees in secret, so that when he comes forth to lead the people of God in worship, he does not come with the burden of personal sin, nor does he come before the people with his channel of communication with the Lord broken.

Penitence and the need for forgiveness should be done daily and not simply ritualistically before serving at the Lord's table. There is a need to be especially aware of the need for such as one goes forth to represent the Lord Jesus Christ and administer from his table.

The third preparatory concern is petition. The pastor should beseech the Lord on the behalf of the people and himself. Sincerely asking for the Lord's blessing to take what he is about to do and be used in the Lord's service is most fitting and in order. Jesus took the bread and the cup and blessed them, giving thanksgiving. We as mortal servants can afford to do no less in seeking divine direction and approval over that which we are about to do.

The petition should be of such a nature to ask the Lord to let his presence be known in the assembling of the congregation and to let his voice be heard through the pastor's words and the music.

The petition for the congregation should be that their eyes be opened and their ears in tune to that which is happening as we participate in the Lord's Supper.

The petition should be through the observance of the Lord's

Supper that renewal and rededication will happen in the life of the church.

The fourth preparatory concern is praise. The Lord's Supper is not a memorial to a dead person, but rather a remembrance of Christ's presence with his people. It is remembering his life, suffering, death, resurrection, and promise of return. We observe the Lord's Supper to remember all that he has taught and commanded of us.

We gather to praise, to celebrate, to shout for the battle that has already been fought, and the victory that has already been won.

We come together at the Lord's Supper—not to cop out or excuse ourselves from the real world with all of its trials and tribulations, suffering, and sighing, but we come to praise our great Savior, for even though he was the lamb that was slain, he is now the conquering Christ.

When the people of God assemble to participate in the Lord's Supper it is a physical demonstration to the world that he that is in us is greater than he that is in the world.

The Congregation at the Lord's Table

"Where two or three are gathered together in my name there am I" *(Matt. 18:20).*

When we assemble to take the Lord's Supper we come not as individuals but as the body of Christ. We come with many members, with many different gifts, and yet we come as one body in Christ.

As we partake of the Lord's Supper we do so as the body of Christ together and as personal members of his body. We maintain our personal responsibility and identify as we come together.

Because this is true, we have to—as the body of Christ, the church, and as personal members of the body—do self-examination on ourselves and church examination on the body of Christ.

We are in no position to come to the Lord's table until we have first acknowledged our unworthiness in coming and yet accept God's grace and mercy bestowed upon us, granting us the blessed privilege to come.

We do not have communion, that is fellowship and relationship with Jesus Christ our Lord and Savior, until we confess that we are sinners standing in the need of God's grace.

The Scriptures must speak for us in preparing the congregation for the Lord's Supper.

> *If we say we have fellowship with him while we walk in darkness, we lie and do not live according to the truth; but if we walk in the light, as he is in the light, we have fellowship with one another, and the blood of Jesus his Son cleanses us from all sin. If we say we have no sin, we deceive ourselves, and the truth is not in us. If we confess our sins, he is faithful and just, and will forgive our sins and cleanse us from all unrighteousness. If we say we have not sinned, we make him a liar, and his word is not in us (1 John 1:6-10).*

The congregation has to have self-discipline. We, as the people of God, have been commanded to obey all that the Lord has told us to do. Christ has commissioned us to observe all things whatsoever he has taught us. Ours is not options or alternatives but obedience to what he has commanded us to do.

Jesus did not say you have the choice of shining for him. He said, "Let your light so shine before men, that they may see your good works and give glory to your father who is in heaven" (Matt. 5:16). Jesus did not say it sure would help the Christian cause if you would love one another, or at least show a little concern about each other every now and then. Jesus said, "By this [love] all men will know that you are my disciples, if you have love for one another" (John 13:35).

We must be a striving, seeking community of believers with our objectives and goals to do all that the Lord has commanded us to do.

When we come to participate in the Lord's Supper we do not come as an option, or because it has been conveniently arranged. We come because Jesus has commanded it of us to do.

The congregation must have personal commitment.

> *Whoever, therefore, eats the bread or drinks the cup of the Lord in an unworthy manner will be guilty of profaning the body and blood of the Lord. Let a man examine himself, and so eat of the bread and drink of the cup (1 Cor. 11:27-28).*

It is the pastor's responsibility to lead the sheep into the area of personal commitment as they participate in the Lord's Supper.

The worshipers coming to the Lord's table must have the awareness and understanding that they are coming because they have decided to follow Jesus as Lord and Savior. We must be daily willing to deny ourselves, take up our crosses, and follow Jesus.

There is the danger that the individual may lose his sense of personal commitment because everyone in the congregation seemingly is going in the same direction. We do not follow Jesus alone, thank God for that, but we do follow him personally. Unity and harmony comes as a result of two walking together, with the same objective and goal.

As we approach the Lord's Supper, we as pastors, need to have a biblical understanding of the Lord's Supper. We should prepare ourselves to lead in the worship experience at the Lord's Supper, and we should teach our people what it means to come to the Lord's table.

MINISTERING AT WEDDINGS

No time will offer the pastor a more opportune situation to become intimately and joyously involved in the life of the parishioners as the time of a wedding ceremony.

This is not a book about wedding ceremonies, social etiquette, or marriage counseling; but hopefully this is a book that will enable the pastor to minister more effectively and efficiently in providing pastoral care in a wedding situation.

As such, my attempt during this section of the pastor as priest will be to focus on skills and tools that will equip the pastor to function as a pastor should.

Significance and Value of Marriage

The Origin of Marriage
The pastor will not function properly unless he has a biblical understanding of the institution of marriage.

1. Marriage is a divine institution, originated, ordained, and ordered by God. This point is vital for the pastor to have a biblical and Christian perspective as to why and what marriage is.

And the Lord said, "It is not good that man should be alone; I will make him a helper fit for him" (Gen. 2:18).

The initiative with man's situation started not with man but rather with God. God said that it was not good for man to be alone. Man did not say that initially. God said it. Man had no desire for a woman, nor even was he aware of the need for one—God saw, God said, God did.

"So God created man in his own image, in the image of God created he him; male and female he created them" (Gen. 1:27-28).

God set marriage apart as a sacred and holy institution that a man and woman could enter. Whenever two people enter the marriage institution, they enter God's institution, not their institution.

Male and female created he them. And God said unto them, "Be fruitful, and multiply, and replenish the earth" (Gen. 1:27-28, KJV).

God ordered his institution by giving a man and a woman the right to coexist and coproduce or procreate as partners with God in his creative process. The man and the woman were and are under divine command, to be fruitful, multiply, and replenish the earth. That was not an option THEN OR NOW: IT WAS NOT MAN OR WOMAN'S CHOICE.

God originated the institution of marriage, he ordained it, and he ordered it. By ordering it, God gave structure, purpose, and meaning to it.

2. Marriage is a spiritual and social union between two consenting persons, agreeing to mutual respect, mutual acceptance, and mutual responsibility.

> Then the man said, "This at last is bone of my bones and flesh of my flesh; she shall be called Woman, because she was taken out of Man" (Gen. 2:23).

This is the spiritual dimension of the marriage institution. God did the creating and the bringing of the woman to the man. God saw the need and moved to meet that need. That is the gospel for everyman; whatever man needs God moves to meet that need, usually before man is even aware of his need.

Therefore a man leaves his father and his mother and cleaves to his wife, and they become one flesh (Gen. 2:24).

This is the spiritual-social dimension of the marriage institution. Two people come together as distinct and different individuals, yet their identities and personalities are bonded together becoming one. Their uniqueness is united through the marriage union. This is the spiritual or God's action that must take place in every Christian marriage.

Looking at the present divorce rate, what God has joined together certainly could not come apart so easily.

3. Marriage is a sexual union, seeking to portray and protect the divine meaning of sex.

"The man and his wife were both naked, and were not ashamed" (Gen. 2:25).

Sex, sexuality, and sexual identity must be understood in the correct biblical context.

Too often our sexual identities have been associated with our guilty identities. We have been erroneously led to believe that whatever is of a sexual nature surely must be evil or sinful.

Let us look at the source of sexual orientation, sexual desire, and sexual fulfillment. The source is God. Now can we conclude or even think of sex in an evil way? I pray that we do not.

God made them, male and female. God brought the woman to man, seeing that it was not good that he be alone, and God was the one who told both of them to be fruitful, multiply, and replenish the earth.

As a pastor you have the responsibility of properly directing and correcting your people as to the meaning of sexuality and the proper way of sexual expression. Sex, in so far as physical expression is concerned, is on the minds of our parishioners, and we must not pretend that it is not there or minister to them as though they were evil for having it there.

Our sexuality is an expression of our spirituality. When the "righteous" brought the woman caught in adultery to Jesus, Jesus dealt with the essence of the situation more than the expression. You who are without sin cast the first stone (John 8:3-11). That was Jesus' way of saying that she was doing what she was doing because of her empty spirituality. You are doing what you are doing in bringing her to me because of your empty spirituality. Jesus told her to go and sin no more. If she was obedient she did not commit adultery again, but she still had her sexual identity, and all she needed to do was to express it in the proper context.

4. Marriage is reciprocal in nature and holistic in scope.

When the Lord God originated the institution of marriage, it was not for the man nor for the woman exclusively but for each other.

Within the marriage union each person has a mutual and reciprocal responsibility to the other. No person can get married alone, nor
can they be married by themselves. Two people come together to
mutually give themselves one to the other for the good of the marriage
union. When I give myself to my wife, I receive from her. When she
gives herself to me, she receives from me. Because we are married, I
cannot do something for myself that will not help or benefit her. If I am
improved, enlightened, enlivened, or inspired by whatever I am doing,
she can become that same way because two have become one.

Marriage has a holistic dimension in its purpose. By this I mean,
in the marriage union, two people are striving to do what is best for the
total person. In the marriage union needs are met; however, marriage
is not need meeting need, but person meeting person.

When the pastor is asked to minister in the marital affairs of his
members, he must come to the situation with biblical understanding
and personal clarity. He need not and must not assume the role of
marriage counselor or wedding coordinator. He is the pastor, and that is
sufficient.

Premarital Pastoral Care

Once again I want to reiterate that the attempt of this work is not
to write a marriage counselor's manual, but the goal is to put in the
hands of the pastor a tool that will help him in shepherding the sheep.

There should be premarital counseling sessions with the couple
getting married. There are several important factors to which the
pastor needs to give consideration.

The Standards of Marriage

1. The pastor should stress the importance of a Christian marriage
as a lifelong union. The marriage union and marriage contract should
be entered with prayerful consideration. Christian marriage is not
something you put on today and take off tomorrow. God never did
intend for married people to break covenant with him or with
themselves. You as a pastor must keep in perspective to yourself and to
the couple that they are about to enter God's institution, and as such
they have to be willing to obey his commands. If marriage was of man's

doing he could set the rules and regulations, but it is not.

Scripture references that could be used are Matthew 5:32; 19:9; Mark 10:12; Luke 16:18; and 1 Corinthians 7:1-16.

2. The Christian marriage should be seen as a life of fellowship (Deut. 24:5). Marriage in a negative way has been depicted as a struggling or an enduring together. Marriage properly understood is a life of fellowship.

3. The reciprocity of the union needs to be emphasized. The Christian married couple is obligated to each other as Christ is to the church (Eph. 5:25). In Exodus 21:10, the husband is obligated to his wife in providing food, clothing, and regular sexual intercourse. Paul deals with this further in 1 Corinthians 7:4-5,39; 1 Thess. 4:4. Also see 1 Peter 3:7. Marriage partners have no legal claims upon the spouse's person and rights (1 Cor. 7:3).

4. The procreation of children enters the picture. The couple contemplating a Christian marriage should have a biblical understanding of their responsibility in childbearing and child rearing (Gen. 1:27-28; Eph. 6:1-4).

5. Birth control is a factor to be considered. The Bible does not teach birth control, but Jesus taught self-control. Man's mastery of subduing the earth has made it possible for him to have dominion even over the procreative process.

6. Abortion is a difficult subject. There is no biblical basis for abortion. All life is sacred, and life and death belong in the hands of God who gave it.

7. Divorce is not God's plan. The pastor should enlighten the couple seeking a Christian marriage that there is no biblical basis for divorce. This writer is acutely aware and shepherdly sensitive to the reality of the human predicament, when "wedlock becomes deadlock." See Matthew 5:32; 19:8-9; Mark 10:12; Luke 16:18. When differences and difficulties arise, every effort should be made for the couple to be reconciled (1 Cor. 7:11). God does not accept divorce but he does accept the divorced persons. He does not accept sin, but he does accept sinners.

8. Adultery is serious. In the Old Testament, adultery was subject to the death penalty (Lev. 20:10; Deut. 22:22). It was looked upon as a form of murder and robbery. Both the adulterer and adultress were

treated as though they were nonexistent or dead.

Jesus' teaching on adultery was that adultery destroys the unity of the flesh and the divine purpose of marriage (Matt. 19:4-6; Mark 10:6-8).

Jesus contended that in the final analysis, a marriage relationship could not be dissolved because it rested on an indestructible basis, God, and therefore could only be disregarded.

Marital infidelity works toward the dissolution of the marriage union by destroying the character of the individual and one's relationship with God and with the marriage partner.

For further help in assisting the pastor in the area of premarital counseling I would highly recommend David R. Mace's book, *Success in Marriage*. In his work, he gives the five basic principles in marriage: choosing, preparing, adjusting, sharing, and maturing. I believe his five major adjustments in marriage are quite helpful in aiding the pastor to give pastoral care on sex, money, work, in-laws, and parenthood. I also recommend Wayne E. Oates and Wade Rowatt's book, *Before You Marry Them*.

Officiating at a Wedding Ceremony

"On the third day there was a marriage at Cana in Galilee, and the mother of Jesus was there; Jesus also was invited to the marriage, with his disciples" (John 2:1-2).

Pastor's Preparational Responsibilities

1. Understand the biblical basis for a Christian marriage. You will not administer pastoral care before, during, and after the wedding ceremony correctly unless you understand the biblical basis for a Christian marriage.

2. See your task as performing the wedding ceremony and not that of doing the marriage. You are there to officiate and preside, giving pastoral direction. You are not there to rule or run a couple's marriage.

3. Have the place, time, and date correctly confirmed. A wedding ceremony is too important to assume when and where it is going to be. I have known of situations where the pastor assumed the wedding was going to be at the church, and the couple assumed that he knew it was going to be some place else.

4. Be dressed appropriately for the wedding ceremony. Preferably dark suit, white shirt, and conservative tie or pulpit robe. You are there to serve, not to style.

5. If the wedding is to be a formal church service, coordinate with the minister of music, wedding coordinator, photographer, florists, and whoever else is involved.

6. When the wedding is to be at the church you should arrive at least thirty minutes before the time of the ceremony. Your presence gives stability and assurance. Also, you may be needed for last minute adjustments and directions.

When it is to be at home, you should arrive fifteen to twenty minutes early. When the ceremony is to be in the home, be especially sensitive to the home environment. Do not ask persons to arrange major pieces of furniture or turn off their radios, stereos, or television sets unnecessarily, until at least the time of the ceremony.

7. Make no last minute changes with the wedding ceremony procedures before checking with the couple. Keep in mind it is their wedding and marriage and not yours.

8. Secure the marriage license before the ceremony. You may want to receive these the day before the wedding. A marriage license is often the last thing on a couple's mind on their wedding day.

9. Have your Bible, marriage manual, or other helps already turned to the pages to be used in the ceremony. There is no reason to be unprepared or unready for the service.

10. Review the whole ceremony before you actually do it, with yourself.

11. Make sure you meet the state or county requirements for performing marriages before you do the ceremony. (In the state of Kentucky, you have to be bonded.)

12. Present yourself as a pastor or minister about to perform a holy and sacred ceremony.

The Wedding Ceremony

The wedding ceremony is a holy and sacred service. The couple, the wedding party, the congregation, and the pastor all stand before the presence of God, about to witness two people entering his holy institution.

There are five components of the wedding ceremony.

1. The Consent—the coming together of two people giving themselves in the sight of God and the presence of witnesses, joining themselves in covenant with God and union with each other.

2. The Ceremony—the actual sacred and holy service where two people come to present themselves to God, asking to be admitted into his holy institution of marriage.

3. The Covenant—the couple's offering up of oaths to God and to each other and the making of vows to be mutually shared and accepted.

4. The Commitment—the pledge of allegiance to faithfully and obediently live together in submission to the commands of God, as expressed through the teaching of the Holy Scriptures.

5. The Community—when two people enter the marriage union they bring their families, friends, and even foes to that union. Christian marriage is not in isolation, but is done in community.

When the pastor performs the ceremony he should come with reverence and holiness. He should see himself as a servant of God ministering unto the Lord's people.

Postwedding Care

The pastor's responsibility is to establish a continual relationship with the couple. He has been instrumental in bringing them into the holy institution of marriage; he must now stand ready to shepherd them. If a church wedding of members has taken place, let this be known to the church community. The support of the church community can be vital in helping a newly married couple adjust and accept the responsibilities of married life.

Seek to shepherd the newly married couple into the activities of the church. If they have not been active before, this is a good time to get them involved. A newlywed Bible or fellowship class could be started.

Sermons and lessons on Christian marriage, the biblical understanding of a Christian family, parent-child relations, all can be helpful to feed the entire congregation.

Church programs and activities ought to be designed with the family in mind. Persons who are single, for whatever reason, can be ministered to in a family-oriented context.

Periodically check with the newly married couple as to the development and progression of their Christian marriage. If done in the pastoral context of love, most couples will appreciate your concern.

Remember the couple in prayer. The prayers of the righteous "availeth much" (Jas. 5:16).

MINISTERING AT FUNERALS

Blessed are the dead who die in the Lord . . . that they may rest from their labors, for their deeds follow them! (Rev. 14:13).

Old Testament Understanding

The first reference to death in the Old Testament (Gen. 2:17) gives the basic orientation for the biblical understanding of death. Here death is punishment for sin. This is seen further in the course of events: when Adam and Eve sinned they were excluded from the garden, the place of communion with God, also from the tree of life which would have prevented the onset of their dying (3:22-23), and were consigned to a life of pain and toil which will terminate in physical dissolution (3:16-19).[17]

It is certainly true that in much of the Old Testament narrative, death is recorded as a universal fact of human experience (see the genealogical table of Genesis 5, with its monotonous repetitions "and he died"), but this is not to say that the writers thought of death as "natural" or as something which was part of God's perfect will for man.[18]

Death viewed as the normal end of life is in both the ancient and more recent portions of the Old Testament. A human life, arrived at its full maturity, is plucked like a ripe stalk at harvesttime (Job 5:26). After a good old age, man, "full of years," is "gathered to his people" (Gen. 15:15; 25:8; Judg. 8:32; 1 Chron. 23:1).

It was most commonly believed that the dead continued to exist in Sheol or in the family sepulcher, but that this was a nondynamic existence, destined to end in a relatively brief period of time. However, certain conditions had to be fulfilled if death were to be thought of as the end of existence: (a) the normal life span must be attained—120 years, according to Genesis 6:3; 70 years according to Psalm 90:10; (b) the deceased must have children to perpetuate his name and on whom he perhaps bestows a testament or words of blessing; (This, however, does not imply ancestor worship.); (c) the dead person must be buried in a sepulcher, for it is necessary to avoid any possibility of his taking revenge and upsetting the equilibrium between the world of the living and that of the dead.[19]

New Testament Understanding

Jesus did not regard death as an obstacle to faith in God or as the crucial dimension about man that must be overcome. Death is a qualifier of man's existence, and as such makes life so precious that there is no equivalent for it: What will a man give in exchange for his life? The answer is clear, not because Jesus believed in the "life principle" or because he believed in the immortality of the soul, but because he saw that life was bounded by inevitable death. The insecurity of life, which the ever present possibility of death represents, should lead to repentance, to a Godward turning of one's life. This is why he can speak of death in various ways when he wants to give urgency and ultimacy to his call.[20]

Jesus Christ has risen from the dead and overcome death. This is the center of the New Testament message and is witnessed to in every part of the New Testament.

All four Gospels record Jesus' prophecies before the event (for example, Mark 8:31; 9:31; John 2:19-22) and the event itself (Matt. 28; Mark 16; Luke 24; John 20—21). It was the love of the apostolic preaching in Acts (for example, Acts 2:24-36; 3:15; 17:31), and the Epistles and the Apocalypse all bear witness to its centrality (for example, Rom. 1:4; 4:25; 1 Cor. 15:4-8; Heb. 13:20; 1 Pet. 3:21-22; Rev. 1:5). He has overcome the devil, who had the power of death (Heb. 2:14). He is the head of the new humanity, the firstborn from the dead (Col. 1:18). He has caused believers to be born anew to a living hope through the resurrection of Jesus Christ from the dead (1 Pet. 1:3).

In Christ, their Head, believers partake of the life of the age to come, and physical death for them is a sleep (1 Thess. 4:15; see Acts 7:59). The sting of death has been removed (1 Cor. 15:56); it cannot separate from Christ (2 Cor. 9:8; Phil. 1:23) and so is not to be feared, and may even be desired (Phil. 1:21-23).

At the second coming of Christ, believers' bodies will be changed and all traces of sin, mortality, and death will be removed. Death will be swallowed up in life (1 Cor. 15:52-57).

At the judgment Death and Hades are said to be cast into the lake of fire (Rev. 20:14), signifying that as God brings in the new heaven and new earth (Rev. 21); the last enemy, death (1 Cor. 15:26), is finally and irrevocably destroyed.[21]

Prefuneral Care

Pastoral Directives

The pastor must deal with the biblical and theological understanding of death. These basic questions must be considered prayerfully and reflectively.

A. What is death?

B. Why death?

C. What is the solution?

The pastor's personal philosophy and theology will have a direct effect on the type of ministry he will render during a death situation.

The funeral director will take care of the physical remains. Your task is to take care of the emotional, psychological, and spiritual remains.

The subject of death needs to be dealt with from a real and healthy position before the immediate reality of death confronts the member. Mary and Martha could have no doubt accepted Lazarus's death differently if they had understood differently. Sermons, discussions, and lessons about a Christian death can be most helpful in building up inner reserves for the awesome time of the death of a loved one.

Once the pastor receives word of a deceased member he should move as quickly as possible to minister unto the family. "God is our refuge and strength, a very present help in [the time of] trouble (Psalm 46:1). The pastor, as God's representative, cannot afford not to move with deliberate speed.

The pastor's responsibility is to care for the living and not for the dead. As Christian pastors we do not have a ministry to the dead, but to help the living. If the mentioning of the dead, the contribution the deceased made, the life that was lived, if any of these can help the living, then use them as a means to minister; and if not, then do not.

The funeral arrangements should be made at a time that is conducive to the pastor and family members. If you contact a family that has just had a member to die, that is not the time to talk about funeral arrangements.

When you do get with the family for funeral arrangements, be sensitive to their requests and advise from a pastoral perspective. Often times when there are disagreements as to the funeral arrangements, the pastor will be used to settle a dispute. Watch and pray to avoid this. A good rule to keep in mind is that you are the pastor, not a funeral planner.

Make no final decisions for the family without the family's consent. Whatever is agreed upon should be done with the pastor and family members working together. If there is something in the funeral arrangement that goes wrong or something in the funeral service that should not have been, the family members, unless they are sensitive, will blame you for their negligence.

Have a word of prayer and Scripture reading before leaving the home, preferably by joining the family members in a circle. The purpose of this is to give a sense of unity and strength, even though a family member has been removed. Your standing in the circle with the family symbolically and realistically implies you are with them and a part of their grief.

How to Arrange a Funeral Service

A Christian funeral is more than the memorial of the deceased. It is a remembrance of what God through Christ has taught us concerning life and death. The services should be consoling to the bereaved, comforting to the living, and challenging and calling forth to the nonbeliever.

Processional—the family enters the sanctuary. You may lead the processional in, or you may receive them from the pulpit. The congregation should stand in respect.

Selection—Music—the minister of music, choir director, or musician for the service should be instructed prior to the service of the order and arrangements.

Scripture—the biblical reading should be appropriate for the services. Just any passage from the Bible is not sufficient.

Prayer—prayed from the heart. No time to impress anyone with your vocabulary or biblical knowledge.

Selection—(Choir, Soloist, Groups?)

Acknowledgements—appreciation of cards, flowers, money, food or other expressions.

Church Paper—(if appropriate) a brief testimony of the deceased member's service to the Lord in the church.

Remarks from Visiting Ministers—briefness should be stressed. (I once knew of a situation where eight ministers were present, and one spoke four minutes for each minister present!)

Selection—usually the favorite hymns of the deceased are sung if known.

Eulogy—offer words of comfort and confrontation.

Viewing of Remains—(only if requested by the family. optional)

Soft Music—creating a comforting, assuring atmosphere.

Recessional

Benediction—usually given at the cemetery after the committal. This is a sample format that can be used with many deviations and adjustments.

Officiating at a Funeral

Prepare yourself spiritually, mentally, emotionally (as best you can), and physically. In most funeral situations you will have at least two days, if not more, to prepare yourself, so there is no reason not to be prepared.

Arrive at least twenty to thirty minutes before the funeral hour. Your presence gives assurance.

Be dressed appropriately. Preferably conservative suit, shirt, tie and shined shoes. Pulpit robe may be worn if desired. You are there to minister in the name of Christ, not show how fashionable and stylish you can be.

Have congregational sensitivity. This would include the environment of the sanctuary: too hot or too cold, not enough seats or not properly arranged, programs, lights, and so forth. The ushers, janitors, or deacons should take care of this, but it is still the pastor's responsibility to see that it is done.

Familiarize yourself with the order of service and the program. Everyone will look to you during the service for the direction.

Make contact with the funeral director to explain any necessary procedures and adjustments. See the funeral director as a member of the ministering team. You are not there to run them, and they are not there to run you.

Conduct your pulpit mannerisms as a pastor, not as a master of ceremonies or a cold "professional" merely doing your job.

Delivery a eulogy. It is not the time or place to try to impress anyone of your preaching skills or your hooping ability.

Do not unnecessarily prolong the services.

If possible, go to the cemetery. Members need their pastor most when they are in the "valley of the shadow of death" (Ps. 23:4).

POSTFUNERAL CARE

Even though Lazarus had died, and the funeral was over, Jesus still came to Bethany to see Martha and Mary. Jesus instructed them to take away the stone. Your pastoral care at this time is to help the members take away the "stones."

Either go by or call the home of the family the day after the funeral. In so many ways the real funeral does not take place until after the public funeral. The lostness, the loneliness, the empty feeling comes often after the benediction has been given.

Remind the family of your continued availability. Do not wait for them to come to you; you go to them. A drowning person does not have time to send out invitations.

Be mindful to have other members of the congregation to give their support. Teach the congregation to rejoice with those who rejoice and weep with those who weep. Walking the road is not so bad, walking it alone is.

Be alert to the possibility that the family or family members may have relapses of the grief process.

Be aware of the family or family members remaining in the fellowship of the church family. Rejection of God's will or not understanding how or why of the death of a loved one is real.

Establish a continual relationship with the family. I have discovered my greatest time of ministering was when the member needed me, and I was there.

Remember the family in pastoral prayer. This should be done both publicly and privately.

In conclusion, there are some practical insights. The pastor's ministry in a death situation is always to the living. You do not need to preach someone into heaven or put them in hell. That is for God to determine, not you.

The pastor goes to console, comfort, convey, and confront.

The pastor has a responsibility to proclaim the word of life in a death situation. Nothing but the biblical Word spoken in love will be sufficient, not poetry, philosophy, or puns.

Be professional but not "plastic," human but not "hard."

Have a means of relieving the grief process for yourself after coming from a funeral or death situation. This may be a family meal with the bereaved family, prayer, silence—by being alone, conversation with your wife, or a change of scenery. You have to take time to come a part. If you do not, you will come apart.

The pastor as priest has a multiministerial responsibility as the worship leader, ministering at the Lord's Supper, baptizing, weddings, funerals. In conjunction with these pastoral ministries, the pastor will be called upon to be an intercessor. How many times has a pastor heard one of his parishioners, or even a person in the community say, "Reverend, pray for me." As an intercessor, he will lead the prayer services and have pastoral prayers for those needing supplications and petitions offered up to God.

His responsibility as intercessor will also be in the area of hearing confessionals. Those who are guilt ridden and anxiety filled will come to the pastor wanting to know that there is a way of forgiveness and restitution.

The testimonial service will be used by the pastor to give the redeemed of the Lord an opportunity to say so. The Lord's people will assemble in the sanctuary of the Lord to lift their voices in praise and song. The pastor will be there to hear and help them tell the Lord Jesus all about their troubles and their victories.

There will be times when the pastor will preside at dedication services. Young babies will be brought to the Lord through him to be blessed of the Lord and to be returned in gratitude and grateful for the Lord giving the child through the parents. This must be done always with the understanding that a child is being dedicated to the Lord and not baptized in Christ.

As the pastor serves as a priest, he will be the bridge builder between God and his people. He will prepare the way for the Lord to come and tabernacle among his people.

6

The Pastor as Prophet-Servant

But so shall it not be among you: but whosoever will be great among you, shall be your minister: And whosoever of you will be the chiefest, shall be servant of all. For even the Son of man came not to be ministered unto, but to minister, and to give his life a ransom for many (Mark 10:43-45, KJV).

SERVANT OF GOD

The pastor as a prophet-servant is a servant of God. He is divinely appointed and not people elected. His commission, his command, his commitment, and his consecration must always be to the Lord who called him. The pastor-prophet is as the Lord said of Ezekiel, "Son of man, I have made you a watchman for the house of Israel" (3:17). As a watchman, the pastor must hear the word at the mouth of the Lord and warn the people according to that word.

The watchman's responsibilities are first, he was called and appointed by God. Ezekiel did not take his prophetic task upon himself, but the Lord called him, commissioned him, and gave him his assignment. The pastor-prophet must be likewise called of God, commissioned by him, and divinely appointed to the task the Lord has given him.

The pastor-prophet stands up for the Lord, speaks for the Lord and even suffers for the cause of the Lord who has called him. The pastor should always see himself as God's man and not the people's man. Many times in the black vernacular, you can hear such expressions in reference to the pastor-preacher, "That's my man," "He's my boy," "He is somebody's preacher," "I'm in his corner." These expres-

175

sions are tolerable if they are expressions of support and appreciation for the job the pastor-prophet is doing. These expressions, however, can be quite damaging to the role identity of the pastor-prophet and to the identity the congregation has of the pastor-prophet if they are taken literally. You as a pastor-prophet are not anybody's man, boy, or preacher. If the Lord has called you, sent you, and supports you, you belong to him and none other. Flattery is OK, but faithful allegiance to the God who rules heaven and the earth is far better.

The pastor-prophet as the watchman must have a vantage point. Ezekiel was placed upon the wall. The pastor-prophet must get on the "wall." The pastor-prophet has to get on the wall of communication with the Lord who has called and placed him.

The watchman's responsibility is to hear the word at the mouth of the Lord and then speak that word in the ears of the hearers. You as a pastor-prophet will never be able to speak for God until first the Lord has spoken to you.

The pastor-prophet needs to get on the wall of prayer. Prayer must never be used as a substitute for not doing, but as a supplement for doing. The pastor-prophet daily needs to be assured that the Lord is with him, that he has not been forsaken or forgotten, and that he is doing the Lord's work and not his own. The flock assembles week after week wanting to know if there is a word from the Lord. The pastor-prophet must spend time in his secret closet to get that word and then proclaim it on the rooftops and in the valleys.

The pastor-prophet needs to get on the wall of patience. He must not move too hastily or blow an uncertain sound. There will be many times when the people will want to go and to do, but the pastor-prophet will have to intervene as a watcher of the eternal clock. There will be times when the people will simply want to circle the mountains with indecision and confusion. The pastor-prophet will have to come forth and say, "Now is the time to go forward."

The pastor-prophet has to get on the wall of moral and righteous living. He will have to incarnate truth, justice, honesty, and righteousness. That will be the only way most of the people will ever come to understand what being a Christian really means. Paul wrote this to the Corinthians, Follow me as I follow Christ (1 Cor. 11:1).

The third responsibility of the watchman is to have a visionary ministry. He must be able to see and perceive. The pastor-prophet must also have these qualities. From his vantage point he must have a visionary perspective. He must be able to see both within the camp and outside. As the pastor-prophet looks within the flock, he should look with the eye of faith and grace seeing realistically what is there and then with the Lord's help seeing what can become of what is there. When Jesus walked by the Sea of Galilee he saw James and John in their boat mending nets. The pastor-prophet must be able to see the broken nets and then not discard them, but by God's grace help to bind them up. The pastor-prophet should know his sheep. There are those in the flock whom he can approach straight forward and tell directly what is on his heart and mind, and there are those who have to be spoon-fed before they are ready to receive pastoral care. Godly wisdom and compassionate sensitivity will help to guide the pastor-prophet in the right direction. The pastor-prophet, as he looks within the walls of the flock, needs to keep his eyes open and keenly aware to those who are wounded, worn, and sad. He must come with a word of hope, reconciliation, and grace to those who are downtrodden. He must see those who are falsely lifted up, boasting in their arrogance, and remind them not to think of themselves more highly than they ought to think (Rom. 12:3).

From the visionary ministerial perspective the pastor-prophet has to look outside the walls of the flock and be able through God's grace to interpret and understand what is going on. The pastor-prophet cannot become so "congregational bound" that he forgets that he has been called by the Lord of the universe to go into all the world preaching and teaching the eternal gospel. The pastor-prophet has to be aware of what is going on outside the walls, because what is happening out there is directly affecting his people on the inside. Once again, he needs godly wisdom to be able to distinguish between that which is just stirring dust and that which can be detrimental to the welfare of the people. The pastor-prophet need not address every issue or feel he has to be in on every policy procedure that relates to his people. The pastor-prophet should know the situations and address himself properly at the appropriate time.

The watchman's responsibility is to report his findings and observations to the people. Ezekiel was placed as a watchman on the wall to hear the word at the mouth of the Lord and then warn the people. He was instructed by the Lord to tell them what he had been told and tell them what he had observed. If they would hear him he was to tell them, and if they refused to hear him he was still to tell them.

The pastor-prophet's responsibility is the same. You must hear the word at the mouth of the Lord and then warn the people according to that word. As you become sensitive to their sins and their sufferings, you must preach God's Word, addressing the issue or the situation. You should never use your position as pastor-prophet to personally rebuke or refute anyone. Your task is not for personal business, but to do the Lord's business with the Lord's people. There are real temptations at many times to reject the people, to renounce them, but the Lord has not called us into a ministry of condemnation; he has called us into a ministry of reconciliation. Ezekiel was told by the Lord that he must warn the people, speaking God's word to them. If he spoke the word as he was told to do, he would be blessed even if they did not hear or obey. If he did not speak the word and the people perished, the Lord would require his blood for the people's destruction. The pastor-prophet's task is to correct and direct, not to condemn or destroy. As a servant of God he must be obedient and faithful, trusting the Lord every step of the way.

SERVANT OF THE WORD

Study to show thyself approved unto God, a workman that needeth not to be ashamed, rightly dividing the word of truth (2 Tim. 2:15, KJV).
That the man of God may be perfect, throughly furnished unto all good works (2 Tim. 3:17, KJV).

The pastor-prophet must be a servant of the Word. To be servant of the Word, he must be thoroughly furnished. To accomplish this pastoral objective, the pastor-prophet must be a student of the Word. He must have a biblically-based ministry. The pastor-prophet is not to get sidetracked into personality syndromes or behavior patterns of expectation. He must be led of the Holy Spirit and check out his fellowship with the Holy Bible. There are pastors who have personality-based ministries, opinion-based ministries, congregational-based ministries, and a whole host of different ministries. The pastor-prophet speaks for God and therefore must speak the Lord's Word to the Lord's people. The pastor-prophet has no words that are exclusively his own. He has only the word of the Lord, and that word is sufficient. If you would just look around you, you would discover that the major root of our pastoral woes is that we have not been obedient to the Word when it comes to pastoral care, pastoral administration, or even pastoral preaching. Hungry sheep (the congregation) will not fight or reject the sincere meat of the Word (the pastoral preaching that is biblically based).

The pastor-prophet needs to develop and maintain study habits that will keep him informed and inspired about what the Lord has commanded of his prophet to do and say. The pastor-prophet should read the Bible with prayerful and studious objectives. He should not read the Bible just to find something to preach about or to memorize certain portions of Scripture to impress someone with his biblical knowledge or lack of it, but he should come to the Word with openness and a seeking heart, asking the Lord to speak to him in his particular situation that he might preach boldly and clearly.

All materials that will assist the pastor-prophet in his ministry ought to be read and considered. This should be done however with the sensitivity that additional reading materials are a supplement to the Bible text and not a substitute for it. The pastor-prophet should read on a daily basis the newspaper and or watch the local and national news. You will not be preaching a relevant and pertinent word to the people in your historical period if you are not abreast as to what is going on with them and around them. You must preach Jesus Christ and him crucified to the contemporary person. The power of Christ is able to transcend cultures and customs, false beliefs and no beliefs.

The pastor-prophet, to be thoroughly furnished, must be a showman of the Word. By this I mean, he must live an exemplary life that makes the Word incarnate among the people whom he serves. You cannot pastor a people by way of remote control. God through Christ showed us that by coming in the flesh. You cannot preach one thing and practice another, talk one way and walk in the opposite direction. To be a showman of the Word, you must study and know the Word and then be willing to demonstrate and declare the Word by your daily actions and reactions.

When Paul wrote the pastoral epistle to Timothy, he instructed him that he who desired the office of a bishop (pastor) desired a good work. He went on to declare to him what the requirements and responsibilities were for a bishop. In 1 Timothy 3:1-9, Paul lists these requirements and responsibilities. He states that the bishop must be blameless, husband of one wife, vigilant, sober, of good behavior, given to hospitality, apt to teach, not given to wine, no striker, not greedy of filthy lucre, but patient, not a brawler, not covetous, one that rules his own household well, having his children under subjection, not a novice; he must have a good report of those on the outside of the church. What requirements, what responsibilities, for any person desirous of being a pastor.

The pastor-prophet must show that he has been called of God and sent by him to oversee his people, by being obedient to the Lord's Word. The pastor-prophet cannot expect to get a hearing or respect as a prophet if he is not showing the people the way to go.

As a servant of the Word, the pastor-prophet should be urgent and instant to preach the Word and do so with profound boldness. The true prophet does not have to ask for permission to speak or apologize for what he declares if he comes in the name of the Lord and preaches God's Word. It is not enough for you as a pastor to read and study and come to some understanding of God's Word and then not be excited and even zealous to go declare that Word and teach that Word.

As a pastor-prophet you cannot afford to be dull, dry, and dead, preaching and teaching about a living God who has the power to lift and love, to seek and to save.

That pastor-prophet as the servant of the Word must reprove and rebuke. You must not become so culturally adapted until you see all things from the people's perspective. There will be many situations and circumstances where the people will believe that what they are doing is acceptable, simply because the majority of the people are doing or thinking that particular way. You as the pastor prophet must stand ever ready to declare that it is not the way. You should never use your position or office to retaliate or reject any person, but you should reprove and rebuke in the spirit of love for the purpose of reconciliation. The Scriptures teach, "Them that sin rebuke before all, that others also may fear" (1 Tim. 5:20, KJV). You do have a biblical base to rebuke, but you do not have a biblical base to condemn.

The pastor-prophet's task is to exhort with all long-suffering and doctrine. To exhort you must warn and give sound advice as to what the Scriptures teach concerning our life-styles, beliefs, and customs. There is no area of a person's life that is off limits to the pastor-prophet. There can be no division of needs or diversification of what the Lord requires. The Lord's Word is adequate in all of life's situations.

The pastor-prophet must be a servant of the Word, studying daily and praying to grow in wisdom, knowledge, and understanding of all that the Lord has commanded for him to do.

He must preach, teach, witness, and work if he will be true to his calling and obedient to his commission. If he has properly prepared himself for the task, he need not be ashamed, for he will rightly divide the Word of truth.

SERVANT OF THE PEOPLE

Then I came to them of the captivity at Telabib, that dwelt by the river of Chebar, and I sat where they sat, and remained there astonished among them seven days (Ezek. 3:15, KJV).

The pastor-prophet has to be among the people that he is going to serve. This involves sitting where they sit. The prophet Ezekiel had to do this, and every prophet must do so in order to become sensitive and aware of the people's needs, hurts, and aspirations.

While sitting among the people, the pastor-prophet should be engaged with more than just sitting. He should be listening to the people. The serious way to understand what people are thinking and hoping is to listen to what they are saying. Listening involves being on the same wavelength or having the proper receptors to receive the message that is being sent. The pastor-prophet has to listen keenly at what is being said among the people so as to address himself in a proper manner. Listening to the people must always be done from a pastor-prophet perspective. You arc not there listening just to listen or just to find out some gossip or some idle talk. You listen to the conversations;

you listen to the relationships the sheep have one toward the other; you listen to understanding and misunderstanding, so that you, through the grace of the Lord, can speak a decisive word that will lead them in the way of the Lord.

As the pastor-prophet listens, he should make sure that his thinking or his actions do not become a direct consequence of what he has heard. There is the danger that the pastor-prophet will develop a reactionary ministry rather than an intentional ministry. A reactionary ministry is when the pastor-prophet speaks only after the people have spoken. He waits until the walls fall, and then he talks about building the walls. He waits until sin has run its course, and then he attempts to stop it. An intentional ministry is where the pastor-prophet has set certain dynamics into operation to create or bring about a desired end. The pastor-prophet ministers with intentions, having goals and objectives clarified. He knows what he is doing, why he is doing it, and who has called him to do it. A reactionary ministry would be defensive in nature while an intentional ministry would be offensive.

While the pastor-prophet is sitting he should observe the sheep. He should see the sheep with both the physical and spiritual eye. With the physical eye the pastor-prophet observes the sheep as they really are. He must understand as best he can why they do what they do, why they think the way they do, why they act the way they do. He must not kid himself or pretend that the flock is not the way it really is. You have to be a realist if you are going to minister effectively over the congregation. There are many situations where the pastor wished that certain conditions did not exist or certain people did not behave the way they do. Wishing and hoping will not avert the real truth.

With the spiritual eye, the pastor-prophet should see the sheep as they might become with the grace of the Lord. Some people only see the mud puddles, but the pastor-prophet must see the mud puddles as potential fertile soil where a great harvest can be had. With the spiritual eye the pastor-prophet ought to see the hand of the Lord at work within and in spite of the people. This is what the Lord had to do with his prophet Ezekiel. He asked him, "Can these bones live?" (37:3). Ezekiel's only reply was, "You know, Lord." This is what the Lord is continuously saying to his prophets as they look out at the "dead bones" of the congregation. From the physical, natural eye the "bones" are dead and without hope, but with the spiritual eye, nurtured by the grace of the Lord, even "dead bones" can receive their strength.

The pastor-prophet should feel the congregation while he is sitting among them. One of the greatest areas of pastoral ministry is the ministry of touch. To touch someone implies I know you are there, I see you, I am willing to reach you, I offer myself to help you, you are not alone. In touching the congregation, the pastor-prophet lets them know he is there to minister unto them, and he is there to reach them. We can be human with the people we serve. We can weep with them that weep; we can rejoice with them that do rejoice. There are pastors who have attempted to hide their humanity or downplay their realness. We as pastor-prophets are real, we are human, and we can afford to touch the people.

The pastor-prophet must not remain sitting among the people permanently. Ezekiel sat among them for seven days, and then he got up and preached. There is a temptation to get where the people are and remain there. You can become so accustomed to their thought and behavior that you become a part of their thoughts and behavior. You are not a people's prophet. You are the Lord's prophet. You must never lose sight of your identity. There will be those members of the flock who will want to mold and shape you, making you into what they want you to be. You must remind yourself first, and then the people that you are not theirs, but you have been bought with a price by him who has called you and keeps you every step of the way.

There are many role models the pastor as prophetic servant will be called upon to fulfill. He must always keep clarified in his understanding that he does what he does because he is a pastor-prophet and not because he desires or ascribes to be something else.

The pastor-prophet will be called upon to be a social activist. For black people, the black pastor has always been the spokesman for the causes and issues of his people. As a matter of fact, if you look around and see who the prominent black leaders are, a good majority are black clergy. The three black national Baptist Conventions, PUSH, NAACP, the former ambassador to the United Nations, present congressmen, SCLC, Black Methodists, and the list goes on and on.

As a social activist, the pastor-prophet should be well informed about the issues and concerns of his people. He should not be on the front line just to be there or just to be seen. He should be there because he has godly wisdom and insight and because the Lord has authenticated and validated him to take a stand for truth, justice, and opportunity for all peoples. He must be the spokesman for the oppressed, the widows, the orphans, the helpless and defenseless persons that make up his congregation and the church community. The pastor-prophet has to beware that he does not get labeled just as a social activist, a civil rights worker, or a humanitarian. He is all of these things, but he is something far greater than the summation of all of them; he is the Lord's anointed, called, commissioned, and commanded to do the Lord's work. He need not apologize for any lesser title.

The pastor-prophet takes his role in the community as a political participant. He should be affiliated with one of the political parties in the democratic process, but he must be careful not to become overly involved with political party identification as opposed to principle identification. The pastor-prophet should not address himself to a Republican or a Democratic issue. He represents someone far greater than either of the two. His concern should be at the principle and people level. Is what is being proposed morally right? Is it honest? Is it fair? Is it God approved? These are the questions the pastor-prophet addresses to himself. The pastor-prophet is an ethical enthusiast and a moral monitor. He stands to speak for God on behalf of God. His calling commissions him, and his divine ordination qualifies him to speak.

The pastor-prophet is a servant of God. That service to God is manifested in obedience to the diligent study of being a servant of the word. As a pastor-prophet is equipped, he is able to become a servant of the people, leading them in the way of the Lord. He is to correct and direct, listen and love and seek and serve the people of God. If he does these things he will shepherd the sheep, and the sheep will enter into green pastures.

NOTES

Chapter 1—The Pastor as Pastor

1. Jay E. Adams, *Shepherding God's Flock*, Vol. 1, "The Pastoral Life" (Grand Rapids, MI: Baker Book House, 1974), p. 15.

2. Ibid., pp. 6-7.

3. This material is adapted from sources cited in an unpublished paper, "Toward a Baptist Philosophy of Christian Education" by Lewis Drummond.

4. Weldon Crossland, *Better Leaders for Your Church* (Nashville: Abingdon Press, 1955), p. 37.

5. Ibid., p. 31.

6. Philip B. Harris and Staff, *Administering Church Training* (Nashville: Convention Press, 1969), p. 12.

7. A. V. Washburn and Melva Cook, *Administering the Bible Teaching Program* (Nashville: Convention Press, 1969), p. 4.

8. Harris, Ibid.

9. Margaret Sharp, *Church Member Training Manual* (Nashville: Convention Press, 1974), p. 39.

10. Jimmy P. Crowe, "Prospecting for Potential Leaders," *Church Training*, Vol. X, October 1973, p. 11.

11. Crossland, Ibid., pp. 31-32.

12. Harris, Ibid., p. 12.

13. Jimmy P. Crowe, *Church Leader Training Handbook* (Nashville: Convention Press, 1970), p. 2.

14. Gaines S. Dobbins, *Learning to Lead* (Nashville: Broadman Press, 1968), p. 40.

15. Crossland, Ibid., p. 22.

16. Harris, Ibid., p. 33.

17. Sharp, Ibid., p. 37.

18. Floyd Massey, Jr., and Samuel Berry McKinney, *Church Administration in the Black Perspective* (Valley Forge, PA: Judson Press, 1976), p. 17.

21. Alvin J. Lindgren, *Foundations for Purposeful Church Administration* (Nashville: Abingdon Press, 1965), p. 23.

22. Ibid. p. 23ff.

23. Ibid.

24. John Sutherland Bonnell, Psychology for Pastor and People (New York: Harper and Brothers, 1948), p. 173.

185

25. Seward Hiltner, *The Counselor in Counseling* (New York: Abingdon-Cokesbury Press, 1952), p. 10.

26. James D. Hamilton, *The Ministry of Pastoral Counseling* (Grand Rapids, MI: Baker Book House, 1972), p. 59.

27. Ibid.

Chapter 2—The Pastor as Preacher

1. Henry H. Mitchell, *Black Preaching* (Philadelphia: J. B. Lippincott, Co., 1970), p. 162.

2. Ibid, 162 *ff.*

3. Henry H. Mitchell, "Black Preaching" in *The Black Christian Experience,* Compiled by Emmanuel McCall (Nashville: Broadman Press, 1972), p. 27.

4. Ibid. 173.

5. Olin P. Moyd, "Elements of Black Preaching," *The Journal of Religious Thought,* XXX, No. 1, 1973, p. 58.

6. Ibid., p. 59.

7. Mitchell, *Black Preaching*, p. 101.

8. Ibid. p. 174.

9. Ibid., p. 72.

10. Moyd, Ibid., p. 57.

11. Ibid., 169.

12. Ibid., p. 54.

13. Mitchell, *Black Preaching*, p. 59.

14. William H. Pipes, *Say Amen, Brother* (New York: William Frederick Press, 1951), p. 139.

15. Mitchell, *Black Preaching*, p. 194.

16. Ibid., p. 112.

17. Moyd, Ibid., p. 62.

Chapter 3—The Pastor as Teacher

1. See Vincent Taylor (*The Name of Jesus,* St. Martin's Press, Inc., 1953) who lists forty-two.

2. See Joachim Jeremias (*Jerusalem in the Time of Jesus,* Trans. by F. H. and C. H. Cabe, Fortress Press, 1969, pp. 233-245) for a description of the

normal process by which one became a rabbi.

3. Robert H. Stein, *The Method and Message of Jesus' Teachings* (Philadelphia: The Westminster Press, 1975), pp. 1-2.

4. Ibid., p. 2.

5. Ibid., p. 8.

6. Ibid., p. 10.

7. Ibid., p. 15.

8. Ibid., p. 16.

9. These are not to be confused with the "I-Sayings" listed by Bultmann, *The History of the Synoptic Tradition*, pp. 150-166.

10. Ibid., p. 8.

11. Findley B. Edge, *Teaching for Results* (Nashville: Broadman Press, 1956), pp. 97-98.

12. Ibid., p. 98.

Chapter 4—The Pastor as Healer

1. Edward Theodore Withington, *Medical History from the Earliest Time,* (London: The Scientific Press 1894), pp. 15-16.

2. Arturo Castiglioni, *A History of Medicine* (New York: Alfred A. Knopf, 1947), p. 29.

3. Solomon R. Kogan, *Jewish Medicine* (Boston: Medico-Historical Press, 1952), pp. 27-28.

4. Isadore Kaufman, "Medicine and Surgery in the Time of the Bible," *Journal of the American Dental Association,* 31:779, June, 1944.

5. George Gordon Dawson, *Healing: Pagan and Christian* (London: Society for Promoting Christian Knowledge, 1935), pp. 20-23.

6. Acts 7:22

7. Maurice S. Jacobs, "Preventive Medicine in the Bible and Talmud," *Transactions and Studies of the College of Physicians of Philadelphia,* 7:175-767, June, 1939.

8. Leviticus 19:2; Deuteronomy 23:14

9. Benjamin Lee Gordon, "Medicine Among the Ancient Hebrews" *Annals of Medical History,* 4:219, May, 1942.

10. A. Rendle Short, *The Bible and Modern Medicine* (London: The Paternoster Press, 1953), p. 27.

11. Gordon, Ibid., p. 27.

12. E. C. Rust, *Nature and Man in Biblical Thought* (London: Butterworth

Press, 1953), pp. 68-71.

13. Exodus 15:25-26
14. Exodus 23:25
15. Deuteronomy 32:39
16. Job 5:18
17. Psalm 41:3
18. Psalm 103:2-3
19. Hosea 6:1
20. Samuel Pordeaux Tregelles, translator, *Hebrew and Chaldees Lexicon to the Old Testament Scriptures* (Grand Rapids: William B. Eerdmans Publishing Co., 1949), pp. 775-776.
21. Proverbs 3:5-8
22. Jeremiah 30:17
23. 2 Chronicles 7:14
24. Dawson, *Healing*, p. 90.
25. Ecclesiasticus 38:1-15. See Herman Berdell, "The Physician of Sacred History," *Transactions of the Medical Society of the State of New York*, 1894, p. 64; Dawson, *Healing*, p. 107.
26. C. S. Lewis, *Miracles: A Preliminary Study* (London: Geoffrey Bles, 1948), p. 168.
27. Adolf Harnack, *The Expansion of Christianity in the first Three Centuries*, trans. James Moffatt (New York: G. P. Putnam's sons, 1904), p. 124.
28. Matthew 4:23, KJV
29. Matthew 8:17, KJV
30. Matthew 9:35, KJV
31. G. G. Dawson, *Healing: Pagan and Christian* (London: Society for Promoting Christian Knowledge, 1935), p. 113.
32. A. T. Robinson, *A Harmony of the Gospels* (Nashville: Sunday School Board of the Southern Baptist Convention, 1922), p. 294.
33. Ibid., p. 34.
34. Matthew 8:14 *ff.*
35. Matthew 8:16 *ff.*
36. Matthew 8:1-4
37. Matthew 8:5-13
38. Mark 2:1-12
39. Mark 3:1-5
40. Mark 5:25-34
41. Luke 13:10-17
42. John 5:1-9
43. Luke 14:1-6

44. John 9:1-14
45. Matthew 12:9-13 and Luke 13:10-17
46. Luke 17:11-19
47. John 18:10 *ff.*
48. Matthew 8:16 *ff.*
49. Adolf Harnack, *Sayings of Jesus,* trans. J. R. Wilkerson (London: Williams and Norgate, 1908), p. 216.
50. Henry W. Frost, *Miraculous Healing* (New York: Richard R. Smith, Inc. 1931), p. 135.
51. In the wilderness temptation, Matthew 4:11; when the Jews demanded a sign, Matthew 12:38-45.
52. Matthew 9:1-8, KJV
53. John 9:1-7
54. Luke 8:43-48
55. Isaiah 35:5 *ff.*
56. Harnack, *Sayings,* p. 216.
57. Mark 2:17, KJV; Luke 5:31
58. Matthew 8:16 *ff.*
59. Matthew 8:1-4
60. Matthew 10:7 *ff.*
61. Acts 2:43
62. Acts 3:1-10
63. Acts 9:32 *ff.*
64. 1 Corinthians 12:9,28
65. James 5:14 *ff.*

Chapter 5—The Pastor as Priest

1. Merrill C. Tenney, gen. ed., *The New Zondervan Pictorial Encyclopedia of the Bible* (Grand Rapids: Zondervan Publishing House, 1977), p. 854.
2. Ibid., p. 854.
3. Emory Stevens Buche, ed., *The Interpreters Dictionary of the Bible,* (New York: Abingdon Press, 1962), p. 877.
4. Ibid., p. 879.
5. Ibid.
6. Herschel H. Hobbs, *Fundamentals of Our Faith* (Nashville: Broadman Press, 1960), p. 115.
7. Ibid., p. 115.
8. Ibid., p. 116.

9. Frank Stagg, *New Testament Theology* (Nashville: Broadman Press, 1962), p. 249.

10. Ibid., p. 249.

11. Ibid., p. 260.

12. *Review and Expositor,* winter 1969—Vol. LXVI, No 1, "The Lord's Supper in the New Testament," Frank Stagg, p. 13.

13. Ibid., p. 14.

14. Ibid., p. 14.

15. Ibid., p. 14.

16. Merrill C. Tenney, gen. ed., *The New Zondervan Pictorial Encyclopedia of the Bible,* Vol. 2, Zondervan Publishing House, p. 70.

17. Ibid., p. 71.

18. *The Interpreter's Dictionary of the Bible.*

19. Liston O. Mills, ed., *Perspectives on Death* (Nashville and New York: Abingdon Press, 1969), pp. 42-43.

20. Ibid., p. 71.

21. Ibid., p. 72.

BIBLIOGRAPHY

Adams, Jay E., *Shepherding God's Flock*, Vol. I, "The Pastoral Life," Grand Rapids: Baker Book House, 1974.

Biersdorf, John, Editor, *Creating an Intentional Ministry*, Nashville: Abingdon, 1976.

Brister, C. W., *Pastoral Care in the Church*, Harper and Row, 1964.

Buche, Emory Stevens, *The Interpreter's Dictionary of the Bible*, New York: Abingdon Press, 1962.

Claypool, John R., *The Preaching Event*, Waco: Word Books Publisher, 1980.

Coleman, Lucien E., Jr., *How To Teach the Bible*, Nashville: Broadman Press, 1979.

Criswell, W. A., *Criswell's Guidebook for Pastors*, Nashville: Broadman Press, 1980.

Cox, James W., *A Guide to Biblical Preaching*, Nashville: Abingdon Press, 1976.

Crossland, Weldon, *Better Leaders for Your Church*, Nashville: Abingdon Press, 1955.

Crowe, Jimmy P., "Prospecting for Potential Leaders," *Church Training*, Vol. X, October 1973.

Dobbins, Gaines S., *Learning to Lead*, Nashville: Broadman Press, 1968.

Edge, Findley B., *Teaching for Results*, Nashville: Broadman Press, 1956.

Faulkner, Brooks R., *Getting on Top of Your Work*, Nashville: Convention Press, 1973.

Hamilton, James D., *The Ministry of Pastoral Counseling*, Grand Rapids: Baker Book House, 1972.

Harris, Philip B., and staff, *Administering Church Training*, Nashville: Convention Press, 1969.

Hicks, H. Beecher Jr., *Images of the Black Preacher*, Valley Forge: Judson Press, 1977.

Hoard, Walter B., ed., *Outstanding Black Sermons*, Valley Forge: Judson Press, 1979.

Jeremias, Lee Joachim, *Jerusalem in the Time of Jesus*, Fortress Press, 1969.

Lloyd-Jones, D. Martyn, *Preaching and Preachers*, Grand Rapids: Zondervan Publishers, 1972.

Manson, T. W., *The Servant-Messiah: A Study of the Public Ministry of Jesus*, Grand Rapids: Baker Book House, 1980.

Martin, Ralph P., *Worship in the Early Church*, Grand Rapids: Eerdmans, 1974.

Massey, Floyd, Jr., and Samuel Berry McKinney, *Church Administration in the Black Perspective*, Valley Forge: Judson Press, 1976.

191

McDonough, Reginald M., *Working with Volunteer Leaders in the Church*, Nashville: Broadman Press, 1976.

McSwain, Larry L., Treadwell, William C., Jr., *Conflict Ministry in the Church*, Broadman Press, 1981.

Mitchell, Henry H., *Black Preaching*, Philadelphia: J. B. Lippincott Co., 1970. "Black Preaching," *The Black Christian Experience*, Nashville: Broadman Press, 1972.

Mosley, Ernest E., Compiler, *Leadership Profiles from Bible Personalities*, Nashville: Broadman Press, 1979.

Moyd, Olin P., "Elements in Black Preaching," *The Journal of Religious Thought*, XXX, No. 1, 1973.

Oates, Wayne, *The Christian Pastor*, Third Edition Revised, Philadelphia: The Westminster Press, 1982.

Pastoral Counseling, Philadelphia: Westminster Press, 1974.

The Psychology of Religion, Waco: Word Books Publisher, 1973.

Powers, Bruce P., *Christian Leadership*, Nashville: Broadman Press, 1979.

Ray, Sandy F., *Journeying Through a Jungle*, Nashville: Broadman Press, 1979.

Richards, Lawrence O., Hoeldtke, Clyde, *A Theology of Church Leadership*, Zondervan Publishing House, 1980.

Robinson, Haddon W., *Biblical Preaching*, Grand Rapids: Baker Book House, 1980.

Rowley, H. H., *Worship in Ancient Israel: Its Forms and Meaning*, London: SPCK, 1976.

Sabel, Mechal, *Trabelin' On*, Westport: Greenwood Press, 1979.

Schaller, Lyle E., and Tidwell, Charles A., *Creative Church Administration*, Nashville: Abingdon, 1975.

Segler, Franklin M., *Christian Worship: Its Theology and Practice*, Nashville: Broadman Press, 1967.

Smith, Archie, Jr., *The Relational Self Ethics and Therapy from a Black Perspective*, Nashville: Abingdon, 1982.

Smith, Bailey E., *Real Evangelistic Preaching*, Nashville: Broadman Press, 1981.

Stein, Robert H., *The Method and Message of Jesus' Teachings*, Philadelphia: The Westminster Press, 1975.

Thompson, William D., *Preaching Biblically*, Nashville: Abingdon, 1981.

Tidwell, Charles A., *Educational Ministry of a Church*, Nashville: Broadman Press, 1982.

Washburn, A. V. and Cook, Melva, *Administering the Bible Teaching Program*, Nashville: Convention Press, 1969.

Wedel, Leonard E., *Church Staff Administration*, Nashville: Broadman Press, 1978.